SEWING REFERENCE LIBRARY®

Sewing for Special Occasions

Bridal, Prom & Evening Dresses

CREATIVE PUBLISHING international
MINNETONKA, MINNESOTA

SINGER
SEWING REFERENCE LIBRARY®

Sewing for Special Occasions
Bridal, Prom & Evening Dresses

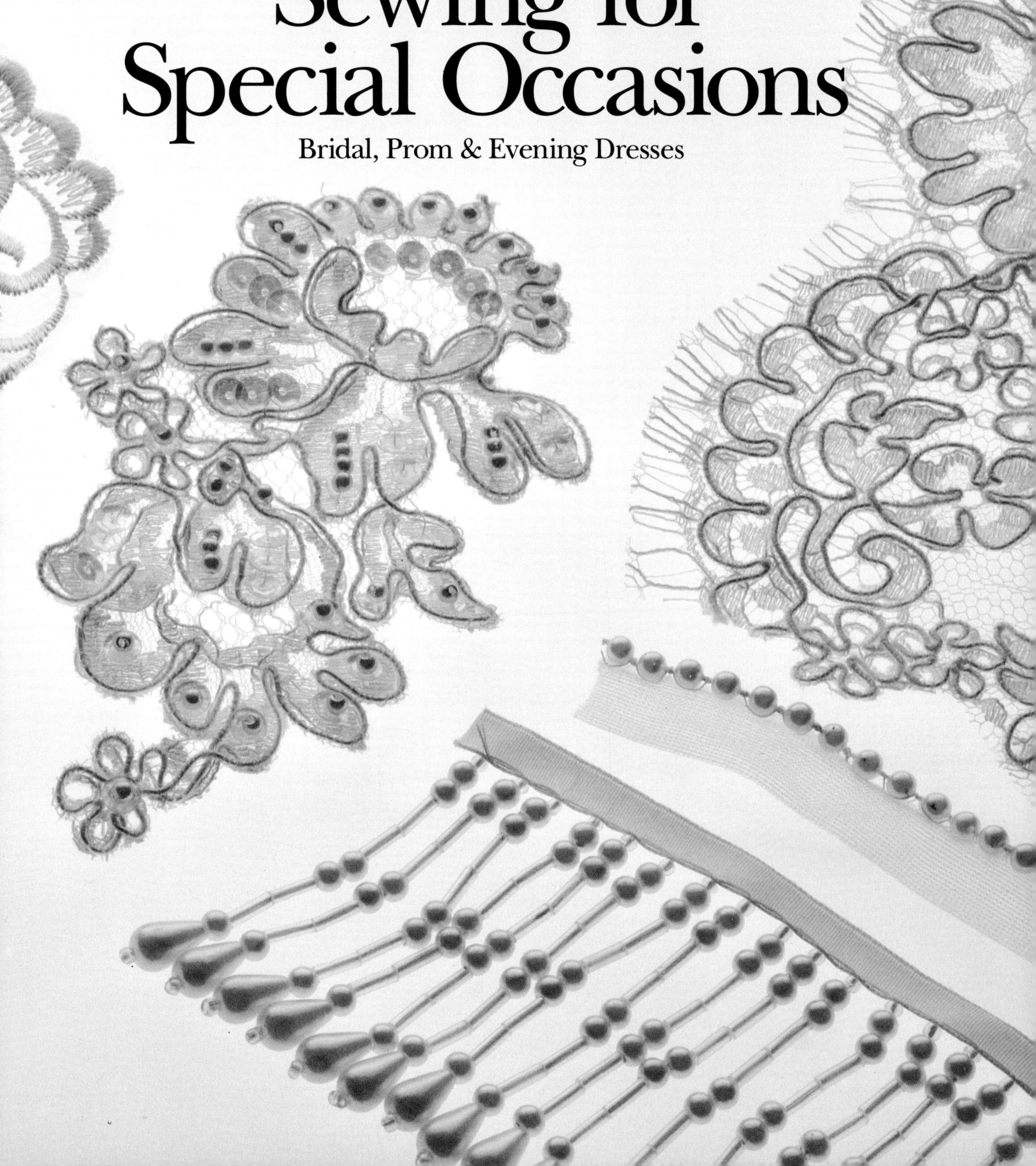

Contents

President/CEO: David D. Murphy

5900 Green Oak Drive
Minnetonka, Minnesota 55343
1-800-328-3895

Printed in U.S.A.

SEWING FOR SPECIAL OCCASIONS

Created by: The Editors of Creative Publishing international, Inc., in cooperation with the Sewing Education Department, Singer Sewing Company. Singer is a trademark of The Singer Company Limited and is used under license.

Library of Congress
Cataloging-in-Publication Data

Sewing for special occasions.

p. cm – (Singer sewing reference library)
Includes index.
ISBN 0-86573-286-8
ISBN 0-86573-287-6 (pbk.)
1. Dressmaking 2. Machine sewing. 3. Wedding costume. I. Creative Publishing international. II. Series.
TT560.S48 1994
646.4'7 — dc20 93-17641

Books available in this series:
Sewing Essentials, Sewing for the Home, Clothing Care & Repair, Sewing for Style, Sewing Specialty Fabrics, Sewing Activewear, The Perfect Fit, Timesaving Sewing, More Sewing for the Home, Tailoring, Sewing for Children, Sewing with an Overlock, 101 Sewing Secrets, Sewing Pants That Fit, Quilting by Machine, Decorative Machine Stitching, Creative Sewing Ideas, Sewing Lingerie, Sewing Projects for the Home, Sewing with Knits, More Creative Sewing Ideas, Quilt Projects by Machine, Creating Fashion Accessories, Quick & Easy Sewing Projects, Sewing for Special Occasions, Sewing for the Holidays, Quick & Easy Decorating Projects, Quilted Projects & Garments, Embellished Quilted Projects, Window Treatments, Holiday Projects, Halloween Costumes, Upholstery Basics

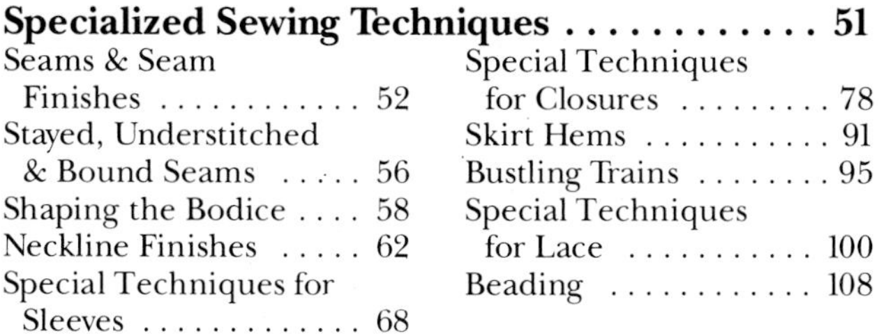

Executive Editor: Zoe A. Graul
Senior Technical Director: Rita C. Opseth
Senior Project Manager: Joseph Cella
Project Manager: Diane Dreon-Krattiger
Senior Art Director: Bradley Springer
Writer: Lori Ritter
Editor: Janice Cauley
Sample Coordinator: Carol Olson
Styling Director: Bobbette Destiche
Senior Technical Photo Stylist: Bridget Haugh
Fabric Editor: Joanne Wawra
Sewing Staff: Arlene Dohrman, Sharon Eklund, Corliss Forstrom, Phyllis Galbraith, Sara Macdonald, Linda Neubauer, Carol Pilot, Heather Smith, Nancy Sundeen
V. P. Development Planning & Production: Jim Bindas
Production Manager: Amelia Merz
Studio Manager: Mike Parker
Assistant Studio Manager: Marcia Chambers

Creative Photo Coordinator: Cathleen Shannon
Lead Photographer: Rex Irmen
Photographers: Stuart Block, Rebecca Hawthorne, Mike Hehner, John Lauenstein, Billy Lindner, Mark Macemon, Paul Najlis, Chuck Nields, Mike Parker, Robert Powers
Contributing Photographers: Doug Deutscher, Ellen Kingsbury, Paul Markert, Brad Parker
Photo Stylists: Phyllis Galbraith, Susan Pasqual
Electronic Publishing Specialist: Joe Fahey
Production Staff: Adam Esco, Mike Hehner, Phil Juntti, Janet Morgan, John Nadeau, Mike Peterson, Robert Powers, Mike Schauer, Tracy Stanley, Greg Wallace, Kay Wethern, Nik Wogstad

Consultants: Helen Adelsman, Joan Bakken, Nicole Balding, Pamela Hastings, Karen J. Nickel, Herman Phynes
Contributors: Butterick Patterns; Coats & Clark Inc.; Emil Katz & Co.; HTC-Handler Textile Corporation; Loomtex Fabrics, Division of Nipkow Kobelt, Inc.; McCall Pattern Company; Olfa® Products International; Simplicity Pattern Co. Inc.; Spartex Inc.; Streamline Industries, Inc.; Swiss-Metrosene, Inc.; Vogue Patterns
Printed on American paper by: R. R. Donnelley & Sons Co.

10 9 8 7 6 5 4

Introduction

For a wedding, holiday party, or prom, you can wear a custom design at an affordable price. Whether you are sewing a bridal gown, like one of the gowns shown here, or a prom or evening dress, like those on pages 8 and 9, this book will be your guide as you plan and sew the gown.

This introductory section helps you identify the basic styles and the popular special-occasion fabrics, laces, nets, and notions. You will also learn how to make a muslin test garment.

The Basic Gown Assembly section gives the sequence of construction for two basic gowns. This section is a guide to understanding the overall process of sewing a gown.

From the preferred seams to the suitable hemming techniques, the Specialized Sewing Techniques section will help you sew the gown. Included in this section are instructions for shaping gowns with boning, neckline finishes, special techniques for sleeves, and several back closures. Also learn how to apply lace, create lace openwork, and embellish gowns with beading.

The Accessories section shows you how to make bridal veils, picture hats, and pillbox hats. You will also learn how to sew a figure-flattering cancan petticoat to support a gown with a full skirt.

Bridal Gowns & Veils

A simple bridal gown in a special fabric, such as brocade, makes intricate detailing unnecessary. Other gowns, with lace openwork or beading, may be more time intensive, but are not necessarily difficult to sew. Learn how to sew an exquisite bridal gown as well as how to bustle the train, using the underbustling or overbustling method. Then create a lovely veil, choosing your favorite headpiece and veiling style.

Prom Dresses

Many styles, from sophisticated to youthful designs, are appropriate for proms. Prom styles tend to be influenced more by fashion trends than other types of special-occasion dressing and vary from one locale to another. Lengths also vary from year to year and region to region.

Depending on the style selected, different sewing techniques from this book are needed. For fitted prom dresses, stayed waistlines are required, and the bodices are often shaped with boning. Sleeve headings are necessary for pouf sleeves. For full styles, sew a cancan petticoat to support the skirt.

Evening Dresses

Formal and semiformal holiday parties call for special dresses, from simple sheath styles to elaborate gowns. The sewing construction of these party dresses need not be time-consuming. Even a simple, basic design can be quite elegant when sewn in a gorgeous fabric. For added glitz and glamour, attach elegant trims to the neckline.

How to Use This Book

Become familiar with the techniques shown in this book before starting to construct a special-occasion dress. Since some of the cutting and assembly requirements may differ from the pattern guide sheet, determine which of the techniques you will use and plan the sequence of construction before cutting the fabric.

In the step-by-step photographs, the stitches are often shown in a contrasting or heavier thread to make them more visible, and the marking lines may be exaggerated.

Selecting a Style

For special occasions, when you want to look and feel your best, choose a garment style that flatters you. Select a silhouette that compliments your figure type and garment details that enhance your best features.

Use sleeve, neckline, and waistline styles to balance the figure. Use details, such as bows, rosettes, and appliqués, to draw attention to specific areas. For example, bows placed down the back of a skirt and train have a lengthening effect, and shoulder details draw the eyes upward. For petite figures, select styles that are properly proportioned. For example, pouf and juliet sleeves should be somewhat smaller.

You may want to try on several gowns to see which styles look best on you. This is especially helpful for selecting a bridal gown style. Go to bridal shops and fashion shows; keep a folder with magazine clippings of gowns you like, noting specific details, such as the neckline, sleeves, or train. Keep in mind where the emphasis of the gown will be; a gown is more flattering on shorter figures if the detailing is at the top of the gown. Also keep in mind that during a wedding ceremony, the gown is seen primarily from the back. Design the back of the gown so it is as interesting as the front.

When sewing a bridal gown, it is also important to choose a white, ivory, or pastel color that is flattering to your skin tone. Whites range in color from those with warm pink or yellow undertones to those with cool blue undertones. Ivories can range from soft candlelights to deeper tones. Try on gowns in various shades or drape fabrics around your shoulders to determine which colors compliment your skin tone.

Silhouette Styles

Three basic silhouettes include the sheath (near right), the princess (middle), and the fitted bodice with a full skirt (far right). Sheath silhouettes are narrow and form-fitting. They may or may not have a waistline seam. Princess silhouettes have shaped vertical seams extending from the shoulders or the armholes, over the bustline, to the hemline, with the skirt curving outward at the waistline. Fitted bodices with full skirts range from those with softly gathered skirts to full, ball-gown styles.

Sheath styles are especially appropriate for tall, slender figures; they are also flattering on petite figures if the garment is properly proportioned. Princess lines and A-lines are slenderizing and create an illusion of height. Fitted bodices with full skirts and basque waistlines are flattering to most figures; the elongated bodice is slenderizing, and the full skirt conceals the hip area.

Selecting Garment Details

From the variety of neckline, sleeve, and waistline styles available, select a pattern that has flattering garment details.

Neckline Styles

Select a neckline style that flatters your bustline, shoulders, and neck. For example, a style with a horizontal line, such as a bateau neckline, can give the illusion of greater shoulder width. Choose a style with vertical lines, such as one with a décolleté neckline, when additional visual length is desired. A sweetheart neckline can minimize the bustline, while a Queen Anne neckline can make the bustline appear larger.

Bateau neckline extends from shoulder to shoulder, curving slightly downward.

Short, gathered sleeves have full sleeve caps and are no longer than elbow length.

Peplum is a short overskirt or ruffle attached at the waistline seam.

Sweetheart neckline dips to a heart shape in the front of the garment.

Sleeveless garment is neatly fitted at the armholes.

Natural waistline is seamed to follow the natural waistline of your body.

Sleeve Styles

Sleeves can affect the overall silhouette of a gown. For example, pouf or juliet sleeves can make the shoulders appear broader, while long, fitted sleeves add a vertical emphasis. Cap sleeves draw attention to the upper arms and make them appear fuller.

Waistline Styles

The waistline affects the proportion of the garment and its silhouette. A garment with a dropped waistline has an elongated bodice, and a style with a peplum has a fuller silhouette. Natural and basque waistlines make the shoulders look broader as they define the waistline.

Modified sweetheart neckline dips to a heart shape, formed by the wrapped front.

Fitted sleeves are long sleeves with little or no fullness; these have pleated fullness at the sleeve caps.

Asymmetrical waistline begins at or below the natural waistline and angles down to one side.

Décolleté neckline may be either a plunging V or a low scoop.

Fitted sleeves are long sleeves with little or no fullness; these have minimal ease at the sleeve caps.

Banded waistline is inset to emphasize or define the waistline area.

(Continued on next page)

Sweetheart neckline dips to a heart shape in the front of a garment.

Pouf sleeves are short, full sleeves; they may be set in or off-the-shoulder.

Fitted waistline without a waistline seam is achieved through shaped princess seams.

Scoop neckline is rounded in the front or the back of the garment or both.

Cap sleeves are short, set-in sleeves that reveal most of the upper arm.

Dropped waistline falls below the natural waistline.

V neckline forms a distinct point at the center front.

Leg-of-mutton sleeves are full and rounded from the shoulders to just above the elbows, tapering to fitted sleeves on the lower arms.

Basque waistline dips to form a V at the center front; the skirt may start at or below the natural waistline.

Queen Anne neckline is high at the back and sides of the neck. It may angle to a scoop or V front.

Juliet sleeves are pouf sleeves with attached fitted sleeves on the lower arms.

Basque waistline dips to form a V at the center front; the effect can be emphasized with beaded dangles.

Clip photographs of gowns you like, noting the details, such as fabric, sleeves, or trains, that please you. For easier pattern selection, compare the photographs to the pattern styles that are available.

Selecting a Pattern

Pattern companies have a variety of special-occasion patterns. However, when looking through pattern books, do not limit yourself to the special-occasion section; a variety of pattern styles from other sections may be suitable when sewn from a specialty fabric.

When choosing a fitted bodice style, you may want to choose one with princess seams, rather than darts, for easier fitting. Princess seams divide the bodice front into three panels, providing ample opportunity for pattern adjustments in the seam allowances.

When choosing a pattern, check to see if lining pieces are included. Lined garments are often more comfortable and wrinkle-resistant. And because seam finishes are unnecessary, lined garments may be faster to construct. Lining the skirt of a gown prevents a net petticoat from showing through and keeps the skirt smooth. Bodices may be lined using the same pattern pieces as for the outer fabric. Some gowns with full skirts will include a separate A-line skirt lining, to reduce bulk at the waist.

To determine your correct pattern size, take your body measurements, wearing properly fitted undergarments. For accuracy, have another person take the measurements. If you are unfamiliar with where to measure, consult the measurement charts at the back of a pattern catalog.

If you wear a bra with a B cup or smaller, select the pattern based on your full bust measurement. If you wear a bra with a C cup or larger, select the pattern based on your high bust measurement. Even if you are a different pattern size in the hip area, it is generally best to choose the pattern based on your bust measurement and make the necessary hip adjustments, or select a multisize pattern. Do not select patterns based on ready-to-wear sizes.

Fitting the Pattern

Fitting the pattern is an essential first step in the construction of a special-occasion garment. A correctly fitted pattern reduces the number of adjustments needed on the garment fabric. This prevents overhandling of the fabric and the need for ripping out seams.

On special-occasion gowns with long, full skirts, the main fitting areas are the bodice and sleeve sections. Pin-fit the pattern to get an idea of how the garment would fit and what adjustments are necessary. For more accurate fitting adjustments, make a test garment (page 20) after pin-fitting the pattern. A test garment allows you to fine-tune the fit and determine the correct wearing ease.

Measure the pattern, and compare the measurements to your body measurements. Make any necessary length adjustments, and adjust the width to fit the bustline, waistline, upper arm, and hipline.

How to Pin-fit a Pattern

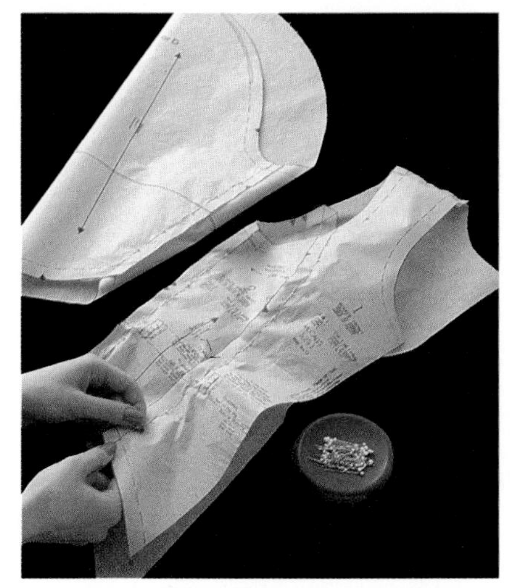

1) Trim excess tissue from bodice and sleeve pieces; press with cool dry iron. Pin bodice pieces wrong sides together, placing the pins on seamlines; overlap princess seams. Overlap and pin sleeve seamlines.

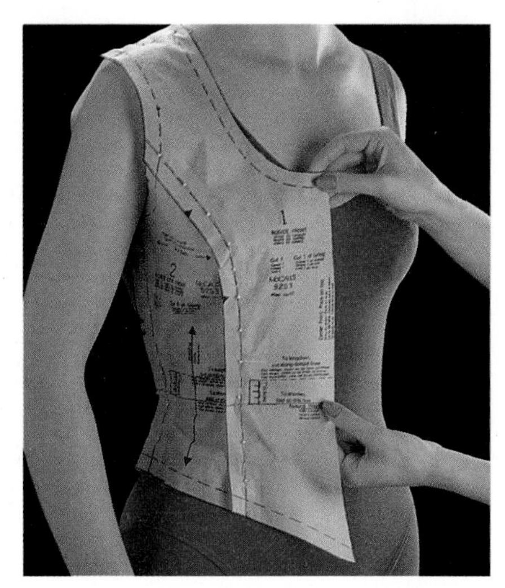

2) Try on the pattern, wearing the undergarments that will be worn with completed gown. For strapless or off-the-shoulder dress, pin the pattern to a leotard or undergarment.

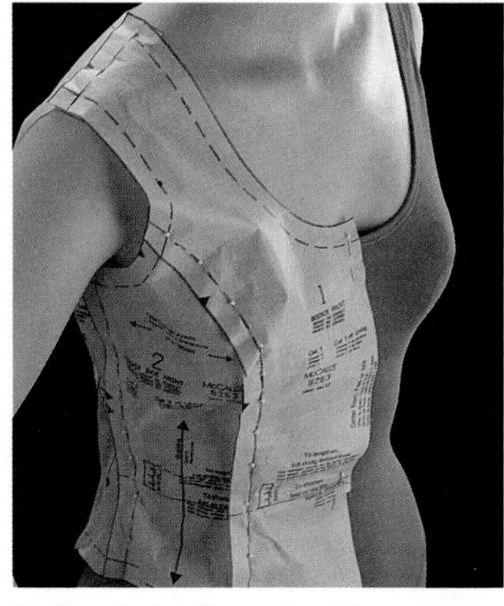

3) Check the fit at shoulder seams; the seams should be centered on the shoulders. Check the fit at the neckline. Make pattern adjustments as necessary.

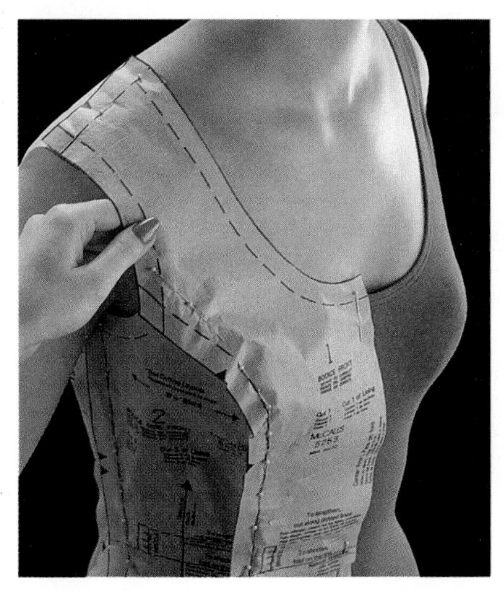

4) Check fit at bustline, waistline, and hipline; adjust the side seams. Check princess seams for correct fit at bustline; adjust (pages 18 and 19).

5) Pin out fullness in sleeve cap; try on sleeve pattern. Check sleeve for adequate length and the desired amount of ease.

6) Pin the skirt pattern to bodice pattern; check for adequate width and length.

Fitting Princess Seams

Many bridal and special-occasion garments achieve their fit through the use of princess seams. Princess seams divide the bodice front into three panels. The seam allowances of these panels can be adjusted to fit the contours of the bust.

There are two basic types of princess seams. The seams may originate at the armholes or at the shoulder seams. The method for adjusting the pattern is the same for either type.

Pin the bodice front and bodice side panels together, and measure the distance from the middle of the shoulder seamline to the fullest part of the bustline curve. Compare this measurement to your body measurement (left). Raise or lower the bustline fullness on the pattern, if necessary, to correspond to your body measurement, if necessary. Then increase or decrease the pattern for a full or small bust, according to your bra cup size.

Bustline is determined by measuring from the middle of the shoulder to a pin placed at the bust point. For accuracy, it is helpful to have another person do the measuring while you stand with your arms down.

How to Raise or Lower the Bustline Fullness

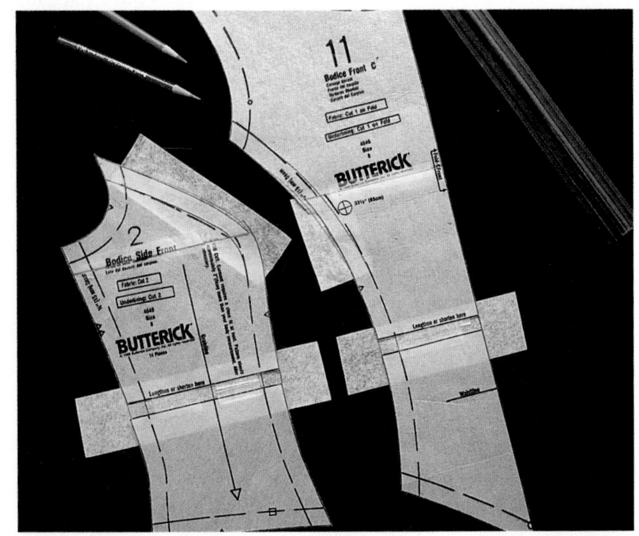

High bust. Draw an adjustment line about 1" (2.5 cm) below armhole, perpendicular to grainline. Cut on line; overlap pattern the amount needed. Redraw seamline and cutting line. To maintain bodice length, cut pattern on adjustment line below bustline, and spread pattern the same amount bust point was raised. Make the same adjustments on adjoining pattern.

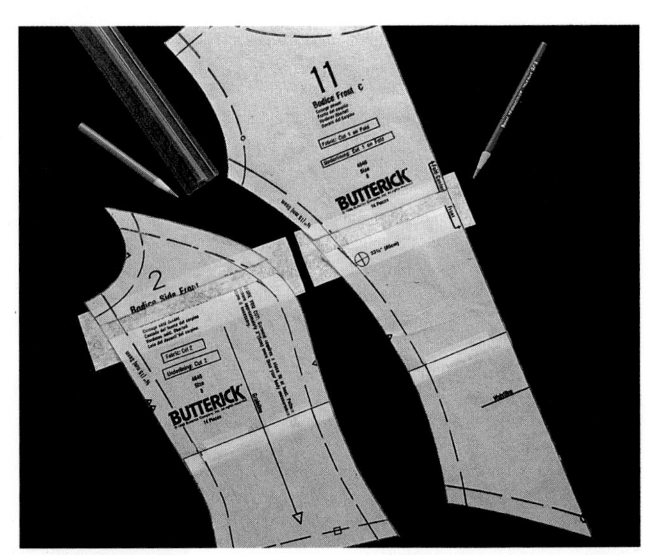

Low bust. Draw an adjustment line about 1" (2.5 cm) below armhole, perpendicular to grainline. Cut on line; spread pattern amount needed. Redraw seamline and cutting line. To maintain bodice length, cut pattern on adjustment line below bustline, and overlap pattern the same amount bust point was lowered. Make the same adjustments on adjoining pattern.

How to Fit a Full Bust

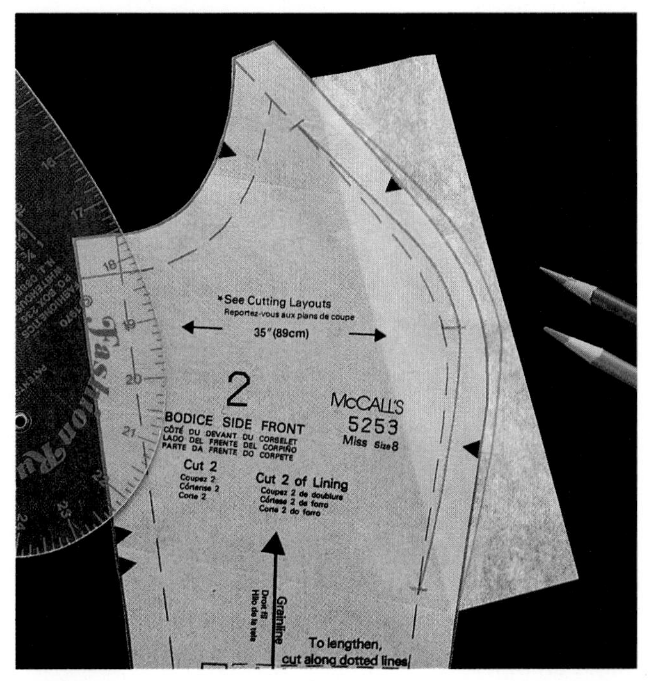

1) Measure out from princess seamline on side front pattern at fullest part of bustline curve, adding ¼" (6 mm) for each bra cup size larger than B cup. Draw the new seamline, tapering to the original seamline about 4" (10 cm) above and below this point. Mark new cutting line.

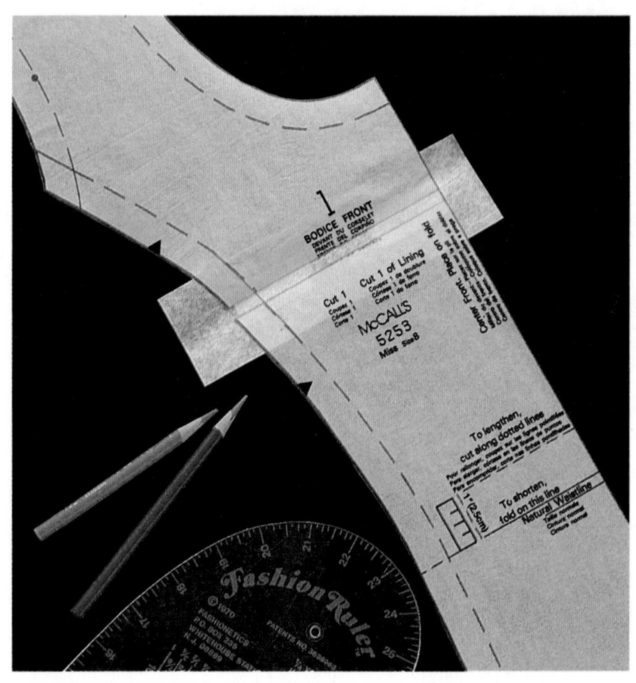

2) Cut bodice front pattern apart between notches, perpendicular to the grainline; spread pattern ¼" (6 mm) for each bra cup size larger than B cup. Mark new seamline and cutting line.

How to Fit a Small Bust

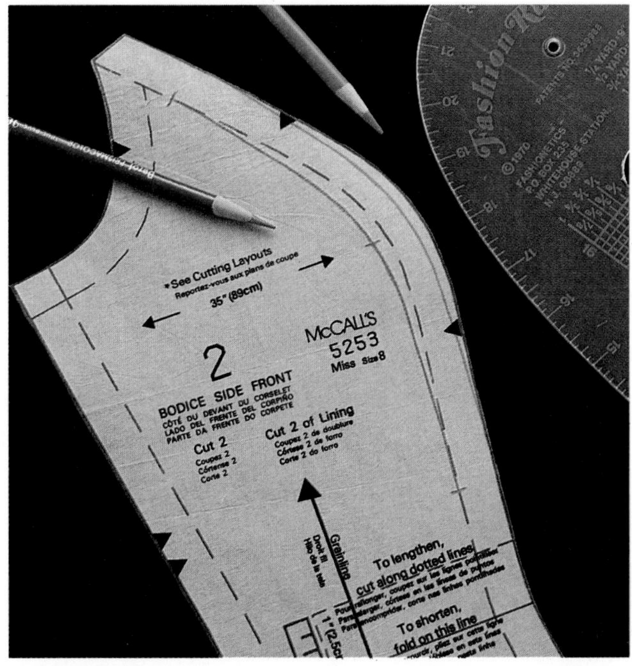

1) Measure in from princess seamline on side front pattern at fullest part of bustline curve, subtracting ¼" (6 mm) for each bra cup size smaller than B cup. Draw new seamline, tapering to original seamline about 4" (10 cm) above and below the bust point. Mark new cutting line.

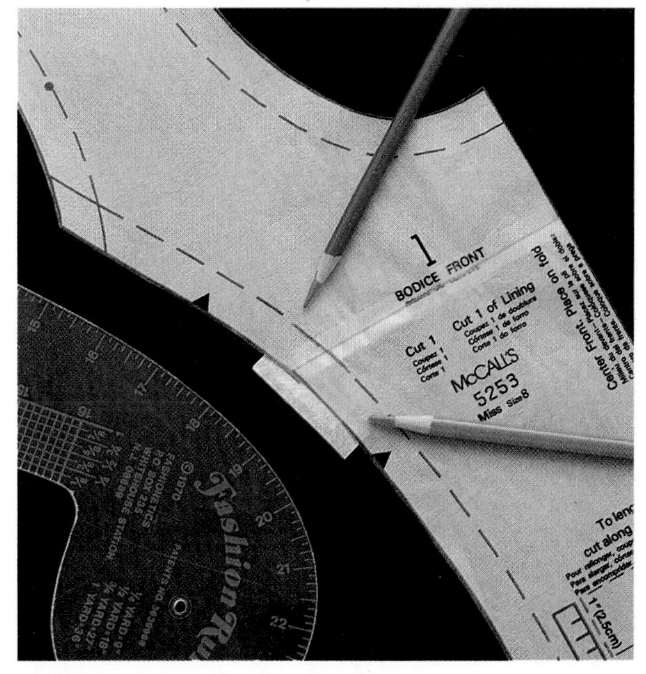

2) Cut bodice front pattern apart between notches, perpendicular to the grainline; overlap pattern ¼" (6 mm) for each bra cup size smaller than B cup. Mark new seamline and cutting line.

Making a Test Garment

Because a fitted bodice is the focal point of many special-occasion garments, a perfect fit is important. Making a test garment, sometimes called a *muslin,* allows you to fine-tune the fit and determine the correct amount of ease.

The test garment can be sewn from muslin or any inexpensive, firmly woven fabric in a weight similar to the garment fabric. For gowns with full skirts, it is only necessary to make the bodice and sleeves; however, if you are unsure of the style, you may also want to make the skirt. For a sheath-style gown, sew a full-length test garment.

When fitting the test garment, wear the undergarments that will be worn with the finished gown. If bra cups will be used, pin them to the undergarments or to a leotard. Wear shoes of the same height as those that will be worn with the gown, because they can affect your posture and the finished length of the gown.

When fitting strapless or off-the-shoulder styles, you may want to wear a leotard so you can pin the test garment to it temporarily at the side seams and the center front. Boning will provide the necessary support to hold up the completed garment.

Fitted, formal gowns are designed with less ease than casual garments. However, be careful not to overfit. The garment should be comfortable for sitting and allow a full range of motion in the arms. When fitting the test garment, make it slightly larger than the fit of the final garment to allow for the bulk of the underlining, lining, and boning.

Make any adjustments affecting the width and the length before correcting other areas. Eliminate any wrinkles that point to problem areas, making sure the grainline hangs straight. Minor fitting adjustments require simple seamline changes. For major changes, you can make tucks in the test garment to eliminate excess fabric or slash it and add fabric for full body curves. These changes must be perfected in the test garment. When the final fit is achieved, transfer the changes to the pattern. Or use the test garment as the pattern.

If the pattern alterations are substantial, you may find it helpful to sew a second test garment, to be confident that the alterations are successful. If you have little experience in fitting garments, you may want to have a professional dressmaker help you perfect the fit of the test garment before you sew the actual garment.

Guidelines for Fitting Gowns

Shoulder seams lie on top of the shoulders and appear straight, without pulling to the front or back.

Set-in sleeves fit smoothly across the sleeve caps. There are no diagonal wrinkles in the sleeve caps, and sleeves do not pull across the upper arms.

Garment fits around the body smoothly without pulling or wrinkling. Reaching does not cause strain across the upper back.

Bustline area is smooth. Princess seams fit properly over the fullest part of the bust; darts point to the bust point.

Garment fits snugly, but not tightly, through the waistline.

Skirt hangs straight and falls smoothly over the hips and abdomen.

Hem is even and does not touch the floor.

Requirements for Wearing Ease on Fitted Gowns

Conventional Gowns		Strapless & Off-the-Shoulder Gowns	
Garment Area	**Amount of Wearing Ease**	**Garment Area**	**Amount of Wearing Ease**
Bustline	2" (5 cm)	**Bustline**	3/4" (2 cm)
Waistline	1" (2.5 cm)	**Waistline**	3/4" (2 cm)
Hipline	2" (5 cm)	**Hipline**	2" (5 cm)
Wrist	3/4" to 1" (2 to 2.5 cm)	**Wrist**	3/4" to 1" (2 to 2.5 cm)

How to Make a Test Garment

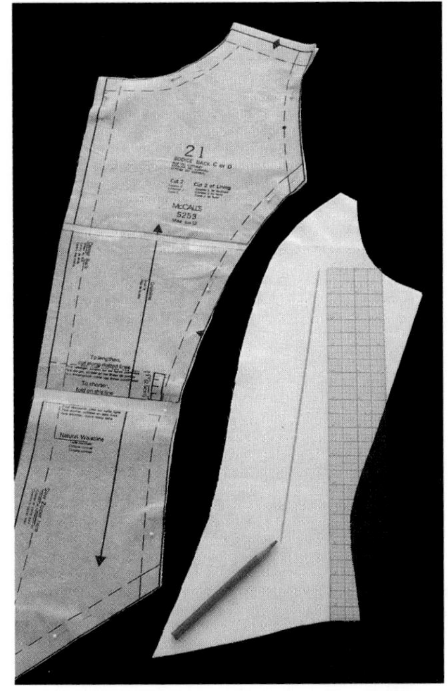

1) Cut muslin pieces, allowing 1" (2.5 cm) seam allowances at center back, side seams, and shoulder seams. Transfer the grainline from pattern to each muslin piece.

2) Stitch on seamlines at neck and center back. Machine-baste muslin pieces together; press seams open. Stitch sleeve seams; set sleeves into armholes, using machine basting.

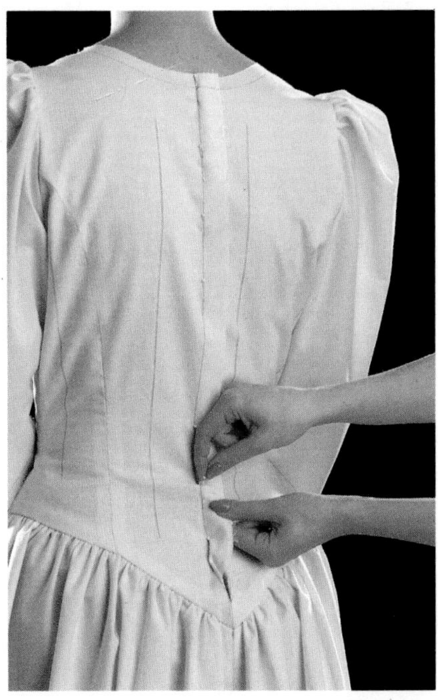

3) Try on test garment, wearing undergarments and shoes that will be worn with finished gown; pin at the center back. Pin strapless or off-the-shoulder style to leotard along side seams and center front. Clip neckline seam, if necessary, so fabric lies flat.

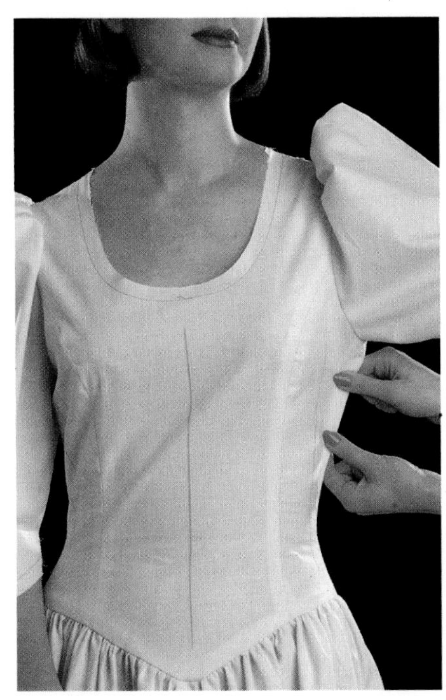

4) Check the garment length, and check the fit through bustline. Pin or release seams as necessary to adjust the fit. Grainline markings should be perpendicular to the floor.

5) Adjust the length of the sleeve while bending arm.

6) Move around in garment; check that shoulders stay in place and that the garment allows for a full range of movement.

Selecting Fabrics

Choose special-occasion fabrics according to the amount of drape or body the garment style requires, using the fabrics that are suggested on the pattern envelope as a guide. For fluid silhouettes, use soft fabrics, such as chiffon or georgette. More structured styles require firmer fabrics, such as satin or taffeta. Velvets and brocades are suitable for simple garments with a minimum of seams. Often several fabrics are used in a garment to achieve the desired look.

When selecting fabric, keep in mind the durability of the fabric and the care and handling requirements. Acetates and silks can water-spot. Slippery fabrics, such as chiffon and georgette, are somewhat difficult to handle during construction. Many specialty fabrics, including velvets, brocades, satins, and sequined fabrics, require a one-way or with-nap layout.

You may want to experiment with the pattern layout before purchasing the fabric. If you are using more than one fabric, or if the fabric width you are using is not indicated on the pattern envelope, you may save money by determining a more accurate yardage requirement than that given on the pattern envelope.

Taffetas

Taffeta (**a**) has a crisp hand and drapes stiffly. It is characterized by the rustling sound that occurs when layers are brushed together. It is available in different weights and is a popular choice for wedding gowns and a variety of cocktail and evening dresses. Polyester taffetas are durable and available in either a shiny or matte finish. Acetate taffetas are available in several weights, or *deniers*. A 180-denier acetate taffeta is very lightweight and is often used for an underlining or lining; it is a good choice for lining full skirts, because it gathers without bulk. A 300-denier acetate taffeta is very firm and is suitable for a form-fitting bodice. Moiré taffetas, also available in several weights, have a watermarked surface texture.

Satins

Bridal satin (**b**) refers to the category of satin and satin peau fabrics. These fabrics have floating yarns that give a shiny surface texture; satin peaus are slightly duller and a little stiffer than satin. Satin and satin peau are available in polyester, acetate, and silk, and in various weights. Silk satin is often referred to as duchess, or tuxedo, satin. Polyester satins are durable and wrinkle-resistant. Acetate satins have a tendency to lose their body if overhandled; they are also weaker and can stretch or pull out at the seams if under stress. For this reason, avoid using acetate satins for fitted bodices.

Shantungs

Shantungs are distinguished by irregular slubs. They may be dull or lustrous. Dupioni silk **(c)** is popular for special-occasion suits because of its body and sheen. Shantung taffeta **(d),** available in polyester and silk, is popular for bridal gowns.

Sheers

Sheer fabrics often used in special-occasion garments include chiffon **(e),** double georgette **(f),** organza **(g),** and organdy **(h).** Chiffon, available in polyester or nylon, drapes softly. It is often used over a separate underdress or camisole. Polyester georgette is more opaque than chiffon and has the look and feel of a crepe. It is very drapable and is popular for mother-of-the-bride dresses. Polyester organza has a crisp hand and is often used for translucent pouf sleeves and as an underlayer on lace bodices and sleeves to support delicate laces. Nylon organdy is stiff and wiry; it is often used for sleeve headings.

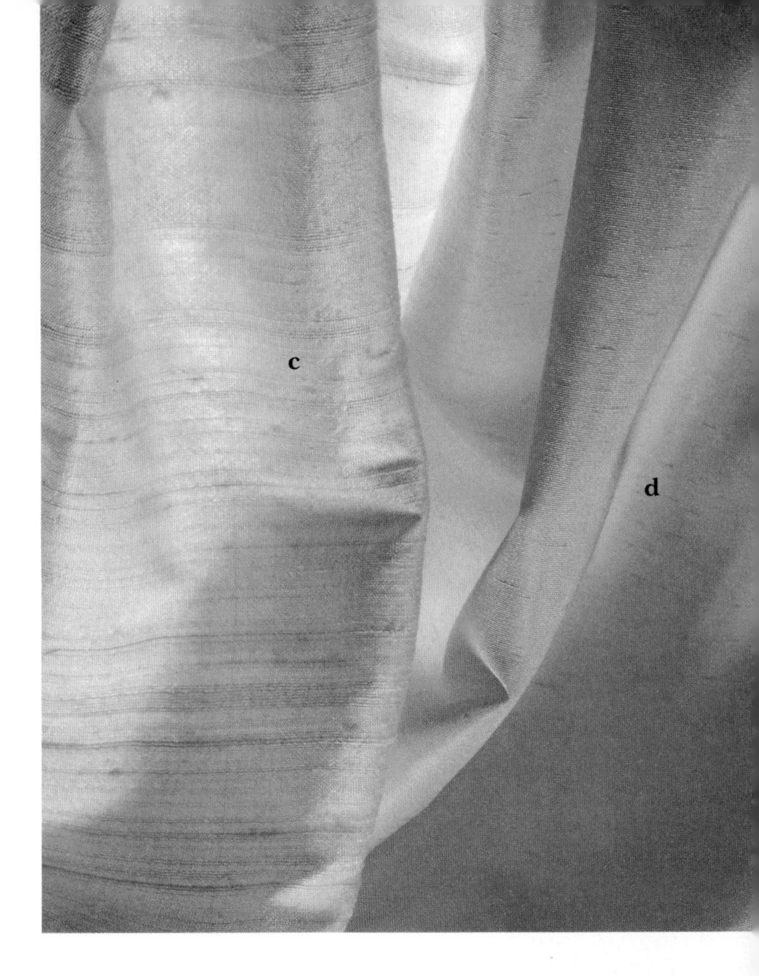

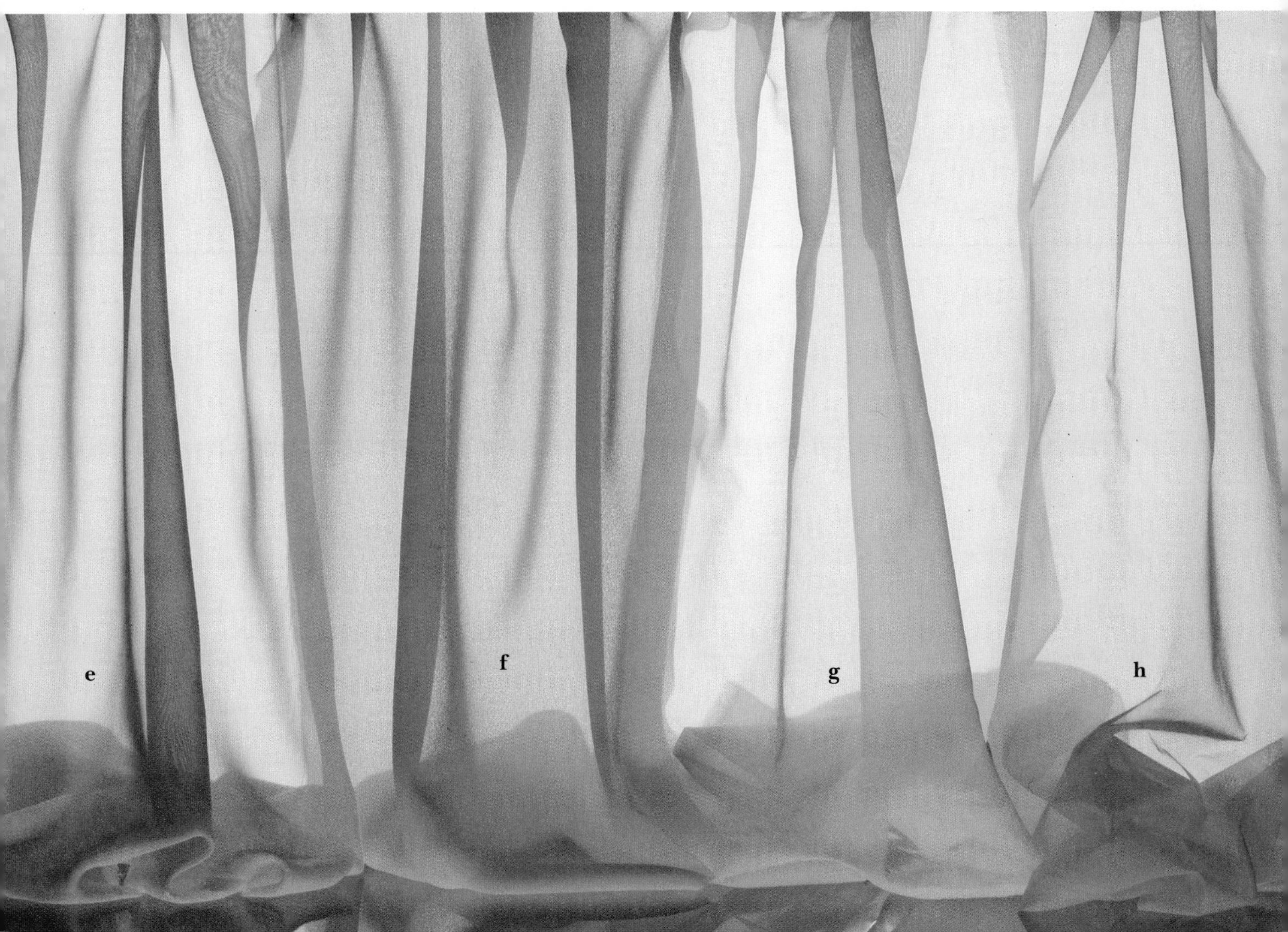

Brocades

Brocades **(a)** have raised, tapestry-style motifs, usually in a floral design. Brocades range from mediumweight to heavyweight. They are generally made in blends, such as cotton/acetate or cotton/polyester, to achieve contrasting dull and shiny surfaces in a single fabric. Examine both sides of the fabric for the pattern created by the floats; many brocades may be cut using either side as the right side of the fabric. Or consider using one side of the fabric as the right side in the main garment areas, and the other side of the fabric for garment details.

Velvets

Velvet is a luxurious fabric with a short, fine pile and a knit or woven back. Velvets include plain cut velvets **(b)**, crushed velvets **(c)**, and panne velvets **(d)**. Rayon/silk or rayon/acetate blends are soft and drapable, making them suitable for gathers and unpressed pleats. Cottons or cotton/rayon blends are stiffer and have more body. Velvets have a nap, requiring that they be cut and sewn in the same direction. Use velvets for garments that have softly draped silhouettes, a minimum of seams and darts, and no buttonholes or topstitching.

Sequined Fabrics

Sequined fabrics may have a knit base or a woven base of sheer or taffeta. Sequins vary in size and may be faceted or flat, with a shiny or matte finish. Most sequins are applied using a chainstitch **(e)** or a three-pronged stitch **(f)**. Sequins that are applied using a chainstitch require special handling techniques to prevent the sequins from coming loose after the fabric is cut. Use sequined fabrics for garments that are simple in style, or as an accent, such as on sleeves or cuffs. Avoid styles with darts, gathers, or pleats.

Lamés

Lamés **(g)** are lightweight woven or knit fabrics with metallic yarns. They are popular for their high sheen and iridescent colors. Woven lamés require delicate handling during sewing and pressing, and cannot handle stress at seams. For this reason, avoid using woven lamé for fitted garment sections. Linings are recommended, because seams in lamé tend to be irritating to the skin. Knit lamés are handled and sewn like any other knit fabric.

Selecting Net

Net fabrics are used for veils, petticoats, interfacings, and garment sections such as sleeves and skirts. The sizing may vary from bolt to bolt; unroll a portion from the bolt to check that it has appropriate body for the intended purpose.

Illusion **(a)** is a fine, delicate nylon or silk mesh that is soft and drapable. Used for bridal veils, it is available in white and ivory, and in a regular and sparkle finish. It is sold in widths up to 144" (366 cm).

Tulle **(b)** is a fine mesh made from nylon yarns that are slightly thicker than illusion. Less expensive than illusion, it is especially popular for gathered net skirts. Its wide range of colors also makes it popular for bridesmaids' headpieces. It is used for bridal accessories, such as rice bags, and as a foundation layer under delicate laces. It is generally available in 54" (137 cm) widths.

Point d'esprit **(c)** is a net with rectangular or circular dots woven at regular intervals. Available in nylon and cotton, it is used for dramatic veils and garment sections such as bodices and sleeves.

French net **(d)** is a very strong, yet soft and sheer, nylon net that is frequently used as a garment section or as a foundation under lace in areas of stress, such as sleeves and bodices. This net has great crosswise stretch and excellent recovery.

Mock English net (**e**) is a nylon net that is not as strong as French net, but has good crosswise stretch and recovery. Unless the net has too much sizing, it can be used as a foundation layer for lace in areas of stress, or for an illusion neckline (page 43).

Nylon net (**f**) is a coarse, crisp mesh with larger holes than illusion or tulle. Available in 72" (183 cm) widths, it is an economical choice for underskirts and petticoats. Because of its wide range of colors, it is often used for bridesmaids' dresses. Avoid overhandling or washing nylon net, because this removes the sizing.

Cancan net (**g**) is the stiffest net available. This nylon net is used for petticoats for full-skirted gowns, where a firm support is desired. It is available in 54" to 60" (137 to 152.5 cm) widths.

Maline (**h**) is a traditional millinery veiling, available in a 22" (56 cm) width and in a wide range of colors. Maline is generally used for the veiling on bridesmaids' headpieces and hats.

Russian veiling (**i**), also referred to as French veiling, is a diamond-shaped mesh available in 9" and 18" (23 and 46 cm) widths. It is used as veiling on millinery such as decorative headpieces, facial veils, and hats.

Selecting Lace

Laces add a romantic look to garments and are easy to work with. Once you are familiar with the types of lace available, you can easily duplicate the look of the gowns in fashion and bridal magazines and bridal shops. Frequently, more than one type of lace is used in a single garment.

When selecting lace, place it over the fabric you are using and stand back to view the pieces. The lace detailing is often more noticeable if the colors of the lace and the fabric do not match exactly. Before you purchase lace for garment sections, it is recommended that you lay out the pattern pieces on the lace to determine accurate yardage requirements.

Types of Lace

Some laces bear the name of the European locality where they were once made by hand from cotton, silk, or linen fibers. Today, many laces are made by machine from cotton blends and synthetics.

Imported laces are among the most expensive, and often have intricate, handworked details. Usually available in narrower widths, many imported laces can be identified by the fringed threads that remain along the edges where strips have been cut apart. Domestic laces, made by machine, are less intricate than imported laces; they are lighter in construction and are made from synthetic fibers. Available in generous widths, domestic laces are economical for making garments with large lace sections.

Chantilly lace **(a)** is a lightweight lace with delicate floral motifs on a fine net background. It is available in yardage and trims. Domestic Chantilly laces are available in 45" and 60" (115 and 152.5 cm) yardage widths and are economical for lace garment sections.

Alençon lace **(b)** begins as a Chantilly lace; a fine satin cord outlines the individual motifs. Available beaded and unbeaded, and in yardage and trims, it is popular for bridal gowns. Although more expensive than many laces, alençon yardage and trims may be cut apart to provide economical motifs and edgings.

Schiffli **(c)** is an imported lace that has a fine net background, embellished with machine-stitched motifs that resemble hand embroidery stitches.

Embroidered organza **(d),** with its sheer organza background, has motifs similar to Schiffli. It is cut and handled like a sheer fabric.

Venice lace **(e)** is made from heavy yarns, giving it a three-dimensional texture. It does not have a net background; picot bridges join the motifs. Usually rayon or polyester, Venice lace has either a shiny or matte finish and is available in appliqués and trims.

Lace Yardage & Trims

Many laces are available in several forms and widths with the same or coordinating motifs. Fabric stores may stock a wide selection of laces or special-order them for you. When purchasing alençon lace by the yard, ask the salesperson to cut around the motifs instead of straight across the fabric. You can then use the entire piece without wasting motifs that have been cut in half.

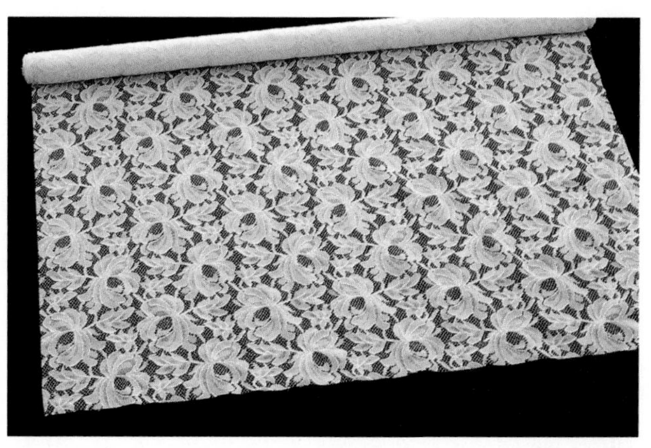

Allover laces have two straight edges and motifs that repeat regularly throughout the fabric. Allover lace can be used for an entire garment, or for individual motifs cut out and used as appliqués. Lace yardage widths usually range from 36" to 54" (91.5 to 137 cm).

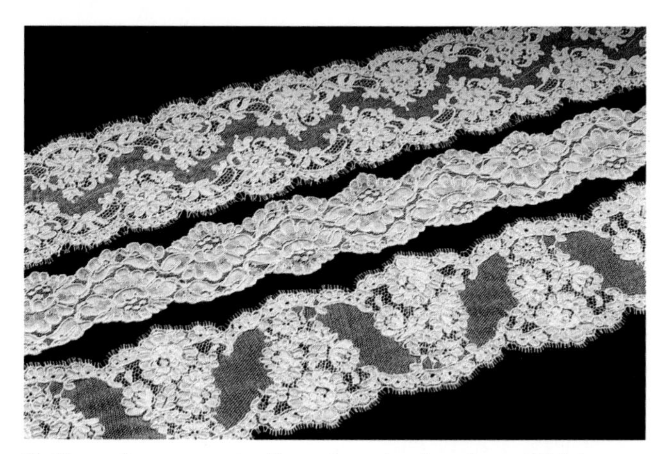

Galloon laces are scalloped on both edges. This versatile lace can be used as a wide border or cut apart so each edge can be used separately. Galloon laces range from narrow trims to wide yardage.

Edgings are narrow trims with one scalloped edge. Widths range from 1/4" to 6" (6 mm to 15 cm). An edging can be used to finish a garment edge.

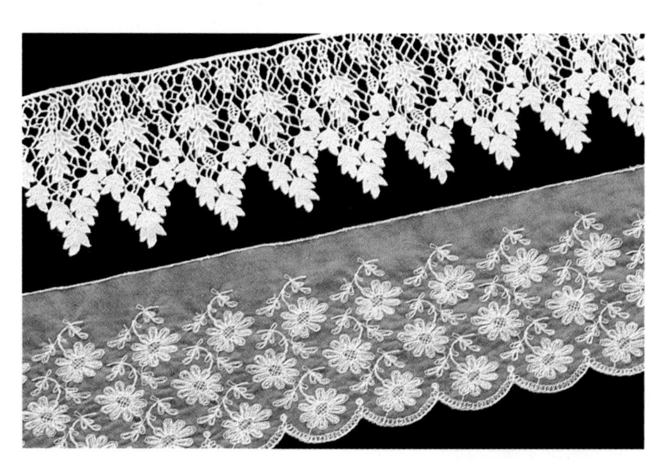

Flounce laces have one straight and one scalloped edge. On embroidered organza, the straight edge is unfinished. Wider than edgings, flounce laces are available in widths from 6" to 36" (15 to 91.5 cm) and are often used for ruffles. Wide flounces may be used for yokes, sleeves, and bodices.

Lace appliqués are individual motifs used as trim. Some appliqués come in mirror-image pairs. A lace bodice is a large appliqué designed to be applied over the bodice of a dress; it usually fits over the bustline and ends at the hipline.

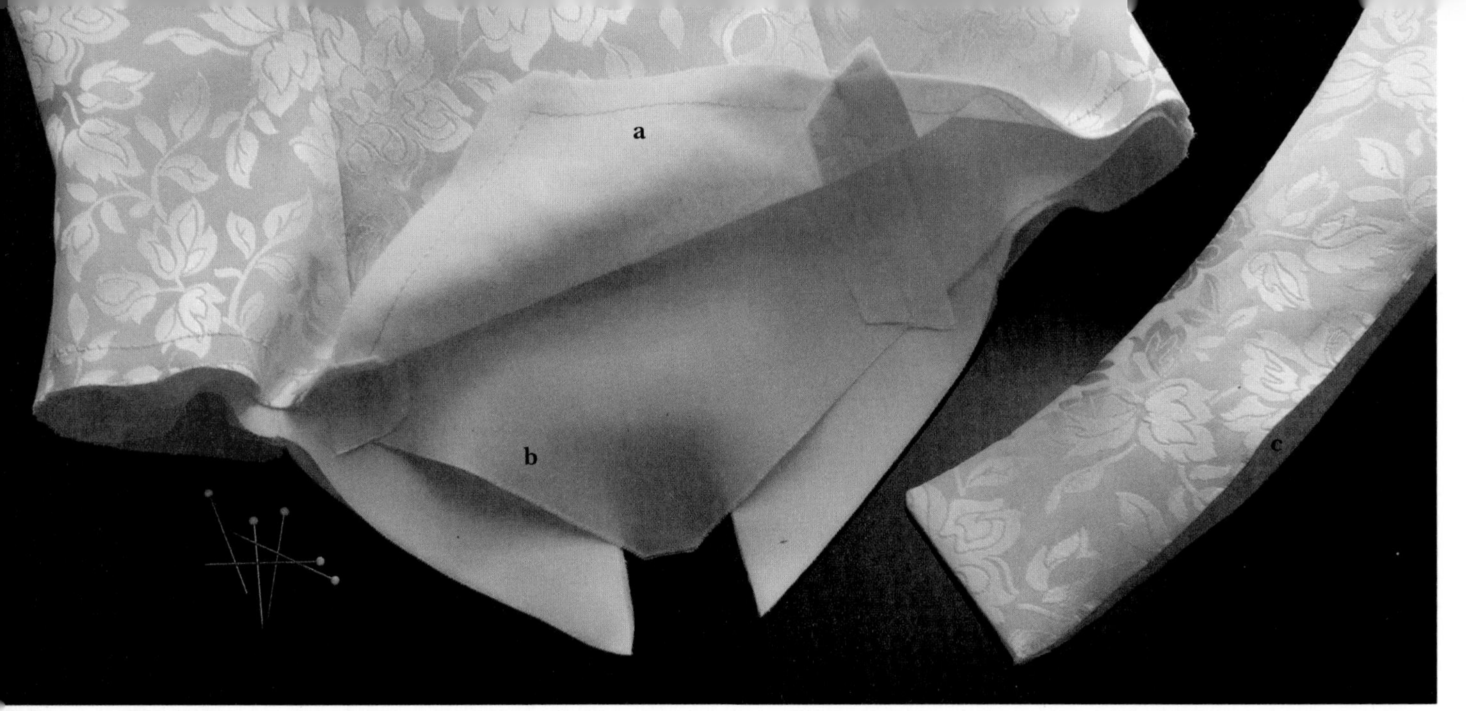

Inner construction fabrics add body to a garment without changing the characteristics of the outer fabric. Outer fabric is supported by the underlining **(a)**; this also reinforces the garment seams. Lining **(b)** conceals seams and darts on the inside of the garment and prevents unfinished seam allowances from raveling. Interfacing **(c)** adds body to garment details, such as cuffs and collars.

Underlinings, Linings & Interfacings

After selecting the pattern and the fabric, select any necessary underlining, lining, and interfacing for the garment; these are the hidden elements that help garments retain their shape. Keep in mind the type of fabric you are sewing and the garment style when you make the selections. Choose inner construction fabrics that have the same care requirements as the outer fabric.

Underlining is primarily intended to support the outer fabric and reinforce the garment seams. It helps to retain the shape of a garment, preventing stretching and wrinkling.

Underlining is cut from the same pattern pieces as the outer fabric. The outer fabric and underlining pieces are basted together, then assembled and stitched as a single layer. Usually the underlining is lighter in weight and softer than the outer fabric, unless some additional shaping is required. Fabrics commonly used for underlining include organza, voile, and batiste. Nonwoven, sew-in interfacings also work well as underlinings. For underlining the fitted bodice of a bridesmaid's or prom dress, use a lightweight interfacing. Use a mediumweight interfacing for underlining the bodice of a bridal gown that will have extensive lace and beading applications; this supports the weight of the lace and beading and creates a smooth-fitting garment.

Linings are used to conceal seams and darts, giving a neat appearance to the inside of the garment.

Linings also cover seam allowances of outer fabrics that may be irritating, such as sequined or metallic fabrics. A skirt or dress lining can eliminate the need for a slip. Linings are sewn separately, then attached to the garment at the neckline, waistline, and armholes.

Select lining fabrics that are antistatic and wrinkle-resistant. Fabrics commonly used for linings include lightweight acetates and polyesters, China silk, and batiste. For a garment with a fitted bodice, a batiste lining may be more comfortable, especially during the summer months. Organza, French net, and mock English net are often used to line lace sleeves and illusion necklines.

In general, interfacing is not extensively used in special-occasion garments. When it is called for, choose one that does not change the characteristics of the fabric. On sheer fabrics, interfacings should be equally sheer; on silky fabrics, interfacings should add body without adding stiffness.

A cool-fuse fusible interfacing, designed for use with synthetic and delicate fabrics, bonds when the iron is at the silk setting. Test all fusible interfacings on a fabric scrap; some fusibles become stiffer after they are fused. If the adhesive comes through to the right side of the fabric, use a sew-in interfacing. Avoid using fusibles on velvet, metallic, or sequined fabrics. Some fabrics, such as organza and batiste, can also be used as interfacing.

Specialty Trims

Many specialty trims are available for embellishing special-occasion garments. Use trims to enhance simple garments or to create glitzy evening wear. Buy motifs that are already heavily beaded, or use beads and sequins to create your own lavish trims. Although some specialty trims are expensive, only small amounts are needed to add drama to a garment.

Beaded and sequined appliqués **(a)** are available for embellishing garment areas, such as necklines, or entire bodices. They are often hand-stitched in place so they can be removed when the garment is dry-cleaned.

Lace appliqués **(b)**, elaborately embellished with sequins and beads, are usually combined with other lace motifs and positioned at prominent areas, such as shoulders and the point of basque waistlines.

Beaded dangle trims **(c)** are available in a variety of designs. The beads are secured to a narrow ribbon or tape. When applied to the gown, the tape is hidden under a lace appliqué or inserted into a seam.

Pearl edging **(d)** is available in single and double rows. It is often inserted into seams at garment edges, such as necklines and sleeves.

Satin piping **(e)** is available in many colors. Inserted into seams at garment edges, it adds subtle definition.

Pearls and sequins **(f)** are available in a variety of styles and colors for embellishing lace and fabric. When purchasing pearls, check to be sure they are dry-cleanable; some pearls disintegrate in dry-cleaning solution.

Rhinestone trims **(g)** are used to embellish spaghetti straps and garment edges. Hand-stitch the trims in place, and remove them before cleaning the garment.

Notions

Specialty notions can help you achieve professional results when sewing special-occasion garments. The design of the gown or dress will determine which of these notions are needed for the desired look.

Notions such as boning, horsehair braid, and bridal bra cups are used to provide support and shaping. Invisible zippers provide inconspicuous closures on gowns, while button looping and satin-covered buttons are used for decorative closures. Bustle buttons, also satin-covered, are sturdy enough to support the weight of the train when it is bustled.

Horsehair braid is used to add body to hems and ruffles. Available in several widths, it is a sheer bias braid that is woven of synthetic fibers.

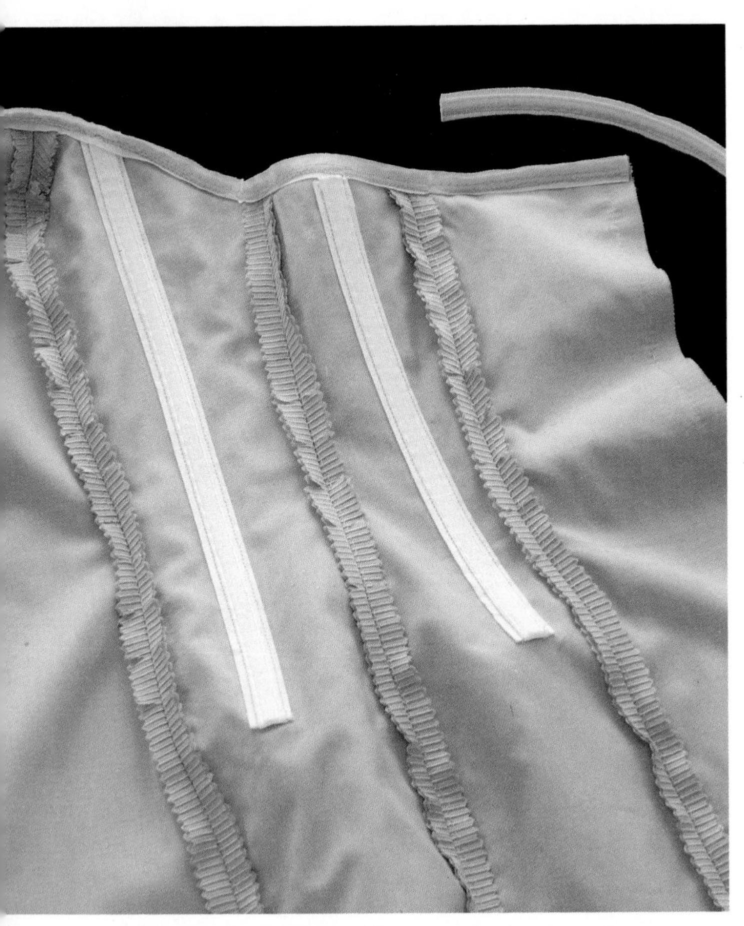

Boning is typically used to create shape and support in the bodice of a gown, and is commonly used for gowns that are strapless or off-the-shoulder. Boning is available in black and white and in several stiffnesses.

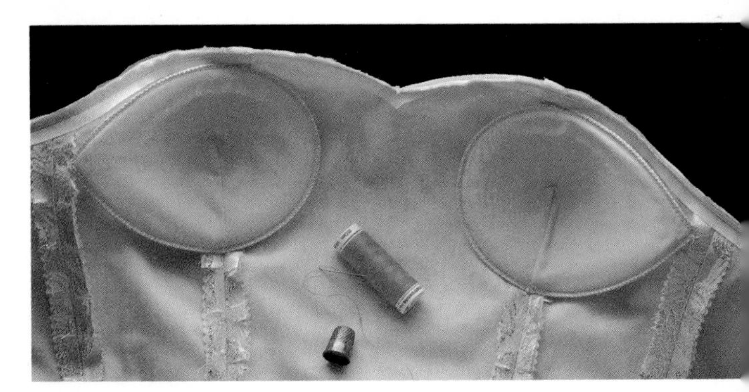

Bridal bra cups are used when support or shaping is desired in backless or strapless dresses, or whenever undergarments might otherwise be exposed. They are generally applied by hand between the bodice and the lining.

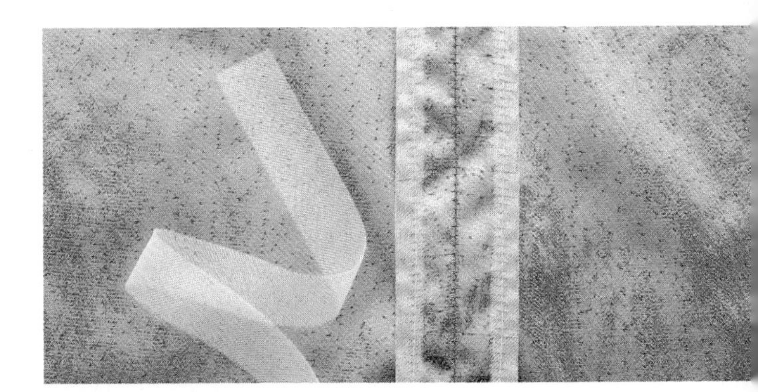

Tricot bias binding is used for enclosing the raw edges of seam allowances on fabrics that may be irritating to the skin.

Invisible zippers provide an inconspicuous closure that looks like a seam. A special invisible zipper foot is required for insertion.

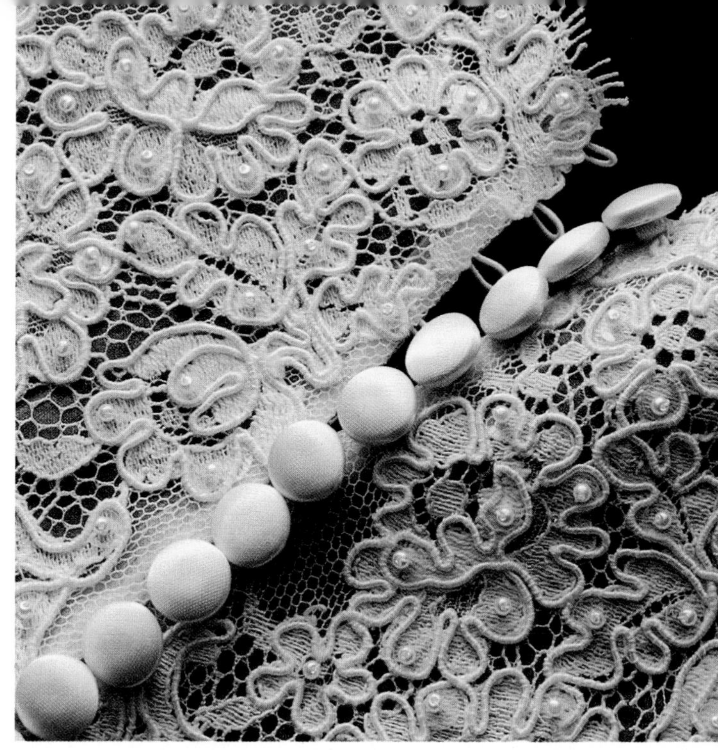

Satin-covered buttons, available in white and ivory, are used for closures on bridal gowns. The shank is covered with tricot to avoid snagging delicate fabric.

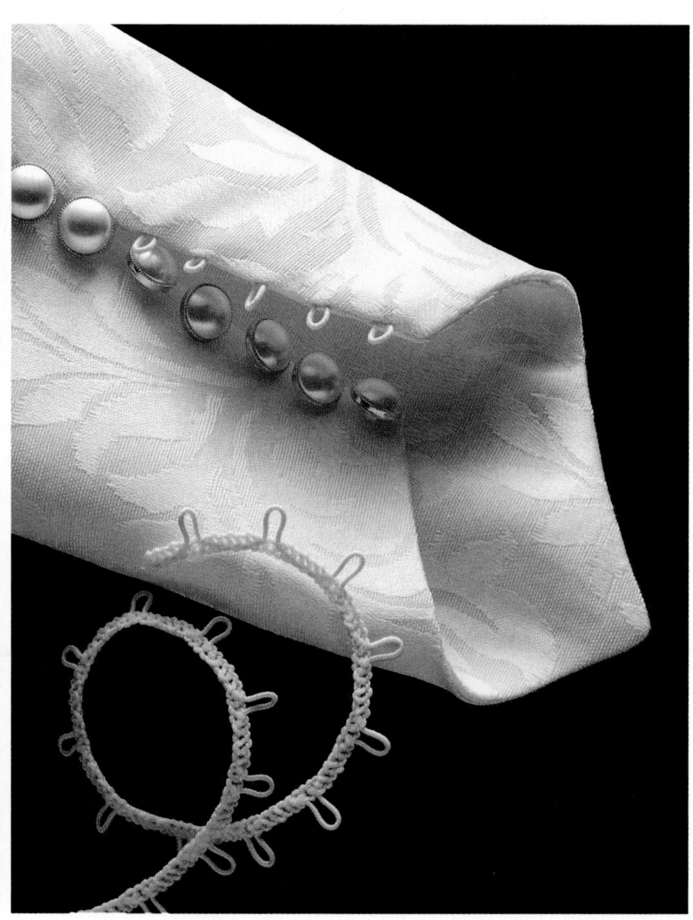

Button looping is used for button and loop closures. In button looping, elasticized or crocheted loops are secured to a braid trim. Button looping is available with loops spaced at various intervals.

Bustle buttons are sturdy satin-covered buttons that are sewn to the back waistline of bridal gowns to hold the bustled train. They are stronger than the standard satin-covered buttons and are available in white and ivory.

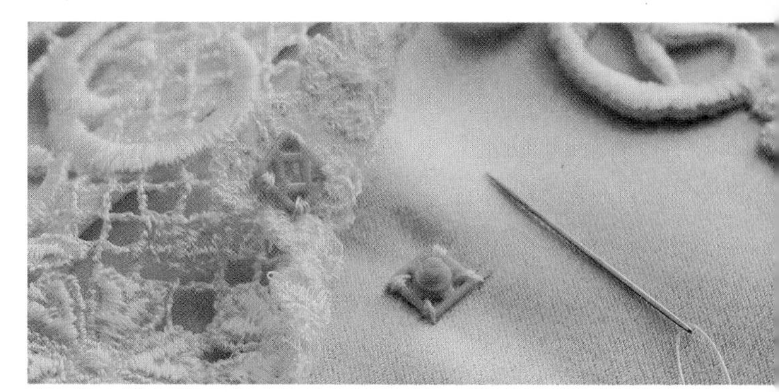

Plastic snaps are available in several colors, and are used on lightweight to mediumweight fabrics. They are used for securing lace motifs that overlap and conceal zippers. (A contrasting snap was used to show detail.)

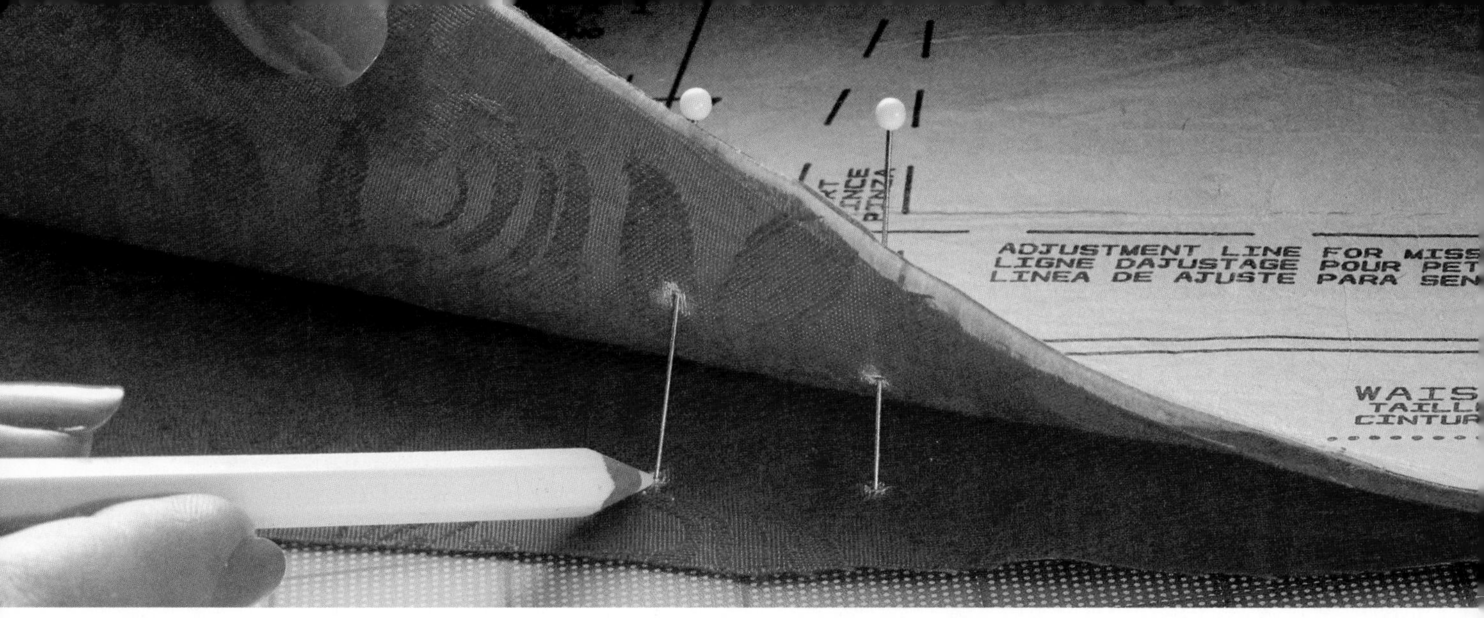

Pattern markings can be transferred to the fabric by inserting pins at the pattern markings and using a chalk pencil to mark the fabric.

Layout & Cutting Guidelines

Careful planning will help you avoid mistakes when cutting specialty fabrics. Before cutting, familiarize yourself with the construction techniques you will be using to determine whether any pattern changes will be necessary. Also determine the direction of a one-way, or with-nap, layout, if required, and whether the fabric needs to be pretreated.

Pretreating is optional for special-occasion fabrics, linings, and interfacings and is often based on the fiber content, the purpose for which the garment is being sewn, and how many times the garment will be worn. Preshrink interfacings by hand washing them gently and allowing them to air dry; or steam press them just before they are applied to the fabric.

When you are making more than one bridesmaid's dress, be sure to cut them alike; mark the wrong side of the yardage for each dress, identifying the direction of the nap or sheen with transparent tape before cutting. If the fabric is to be pretreated, make sure the yardage for every dress is pretreated in the same manner.

Cut bodice pieces with 1" (2.5 cm) seam allowances at the side seams, to allow for minor fitting adjustments. You may also want to allow 1" (2.5 cm) at the center back, especially if you are working with fabrics that are ravel-prone. Allow a 3" to 4" (7.5 to 10 cm) hem allowance on full skirts that will be worn with a cancan petticoat; this allows extra length that may be needed because of the fullness of the petticoat. A hem allowance of 5/8" (1.5 cm) is sufficient in the train area.

A rotary cutter and cutting mat work best for cutting sheer and silky fabrics; the rotary blade cuts fabric edges neatly without shifting the fabric. Bent-handled dressmaker's shears also work well. Avoid using your best shears on sequined fabrics, which will quickly dull the blades. Allow sufficient workspace to spread out the pattern pieces. Pattern pieces can be held in place with pins or weights. When pinning into fine fabric, make sure the pins do not mar the fabric; you may need to pin within the seam allowances. Use superfine pins to avoid snagging the fabric.

Use a one-way pattern layout for all fabrics that have luster or shine, such as satins, taffetas, and brocades, to ensure uniform color shading in the finished garment. Some fabrics look lighter or brighter in one direction; decide which shading you prefer.

The color of sequined fabrics is affected by the way the sequins lie; these fabrics should be cut with the sequins running down toward the lower edge of the garment. The sequins often come loose once the fabric is cut; remove the sequins from the seam allowances and secure the threads as on page 54 before stitching the seams in the garment.

Garment pieces from lightweight laces, such as Chantilly or embroidered organza, are generally cut with standard seam allowances. Overlapped seams are used for heavier laces, like alençon. Cut alençon lace sleeves as on page 75; cut alençon lace bodices as on page 103.

Pattern notches can be marked on most fabrics by making 1/8" (3 mm) clips in the seam allowances. Make additional pattern markings, such as darts, with tailor's tacks to prevent damaging the fabric. Chalk may also be used on heavier fabrics, such as brocades and velvets; test the chalk on the fabric to be sure it can be removed. Avoid using temporary marking pens, which may stain some fabrics.

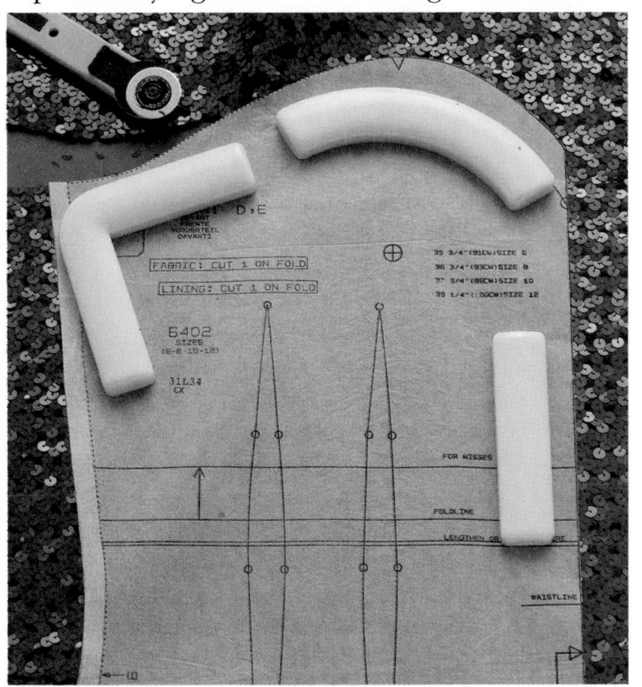

Sequined fabric. Use a one-way layout, and cut a single layer of fabric, right side up. Sequins should run toward the lower edge of garment. Use weights to avoid pinning into sequins. Cut facings from a lightweight lining fabric to reduce bulk and to prevent the sequins from irritating the skin.

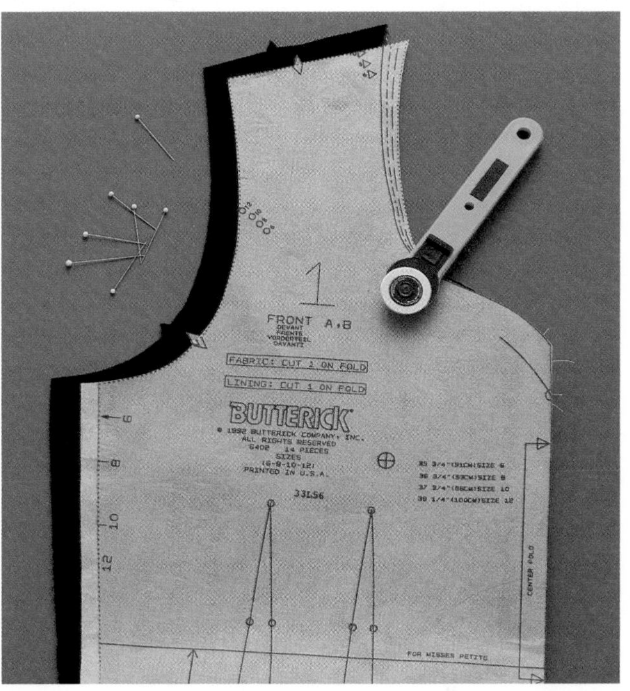

Velvet fabric. Use a one-way layout, and cut a single layer to prevent the fabric from shifting. Cut around pattern notches, because clipping seam allowances could cause a tear. Remove pins immediately after cutting out pattern to prevent imprints on pile. Cut facings from lightweight lining fabric to reduce bulk.

Sheer or silky fabric. Place a very slippery or thin fabric between layers of tissue paper for better control. Place tissue paper on the cutting surface, and place the fabric and pattern on tissue paper; pin through all layers, within the seam allowances. Cut through all layers.

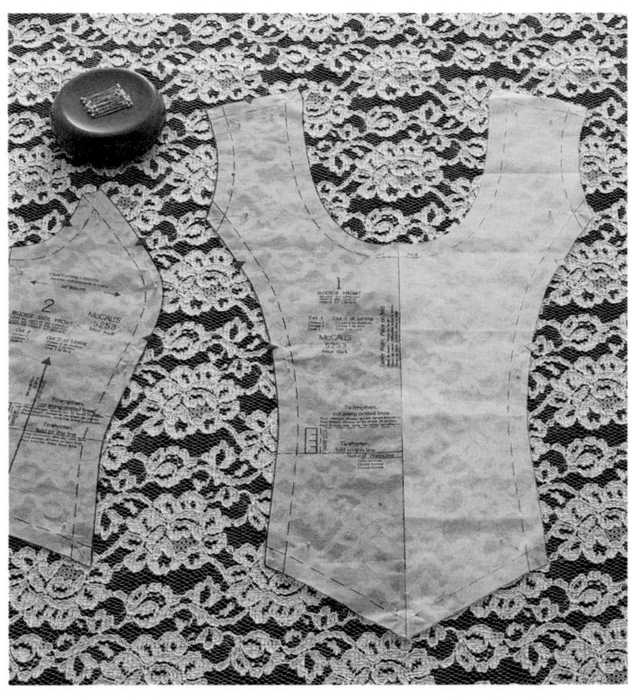

Lace. Draw full-size pattern pieces, using tissue paper or sheer nonwoven interfacing. Lay out the pattern on a single layer of lace, centering or balancing the motifs; match the motifs at seamlines. Use long pins to secure the pattern.

Preserve the nap of velvets by placing fabric right side down on needleboard, textured towel, or velvet scrap.

Pressing Techniques

Pressing as you sew is important for specialty fabrics. It is equally important to avoid overpressing, because many fabrics are easily damaged by heat and steam. Overpressing can also result in seam imprints on the right side of the garment.

Test the pressing techniques on fabric scraps. Begin with a low temperature setting, and raise the setting as needed for desired results. Check to see how the fabric reacts to steam. Use caution when steaming acetates and silks, because they tend to water-spot. Avoid steam on sequined and metallic fabrics, because steam removes the surface luster. Use a cotton ironing board cover; covers that reflect the heat increase the risk of shrinking the fabric, melting heat-sensitive fibers, and leaving shine marks from the iron.

When pressing fabrics, glide the iron over the fabric, using little or no pressure. Some fabrics, such as velvets, may be shaped using a steam setting without touching the iron to the fabric. Lightly finger-press the seam open after steaming. Press fabrics from the wrong side whenever possible. If it is necessary to press from the right side, protect the fabric with an iron guard or a press cloth. Also use an iron guard or a press cloth when pressing lace or other fragile fabrics from the wrong side.

Tips for Pressing Specialty Fabrics

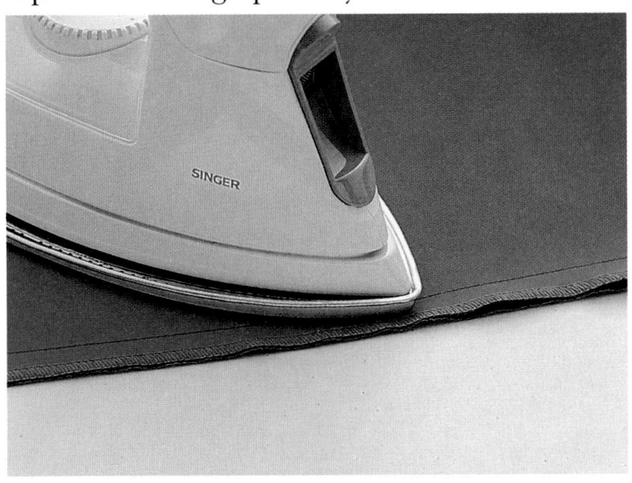

Press seams flat on satin and taffeta before pressing them open. Pressing the seam flat embeds the stitches for a smooth seam.

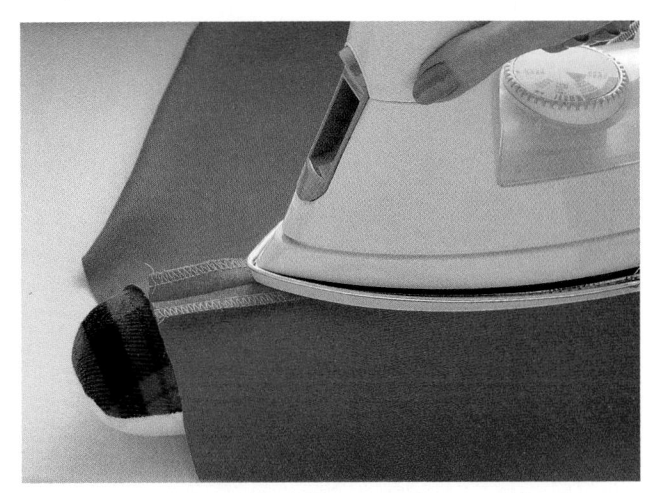

Use a seam roll to press the seams open without imprinting seam edges on right side of garment.

Use a tailor's ham to press any shaped areas, such as curved seams, darts, or sleeve caps.

Place narrow strips of paper under darts and pleats to avoid imprinting the edges on the right side.

Protect delicate fabrics from excessive heat and steam by using a press cloth. A see-through press cloth allows you to avoid pressing over embellishments.

Press laces right side down on a well-padded surface to preserve the texture of the lace. Use a press cloth to prevent the tip of the iron from catching on the lace or tearing it.

Basic Gown Assembly

Three Stages of Sewing a Gown

1) Assembling a bodice. The bodice is the garment section that has the most detail and fitting concerns. Lace, sequins, or beads are usually applied to the bodice at this stage for ease in handling.

Although gown construction may appear complicated or intricate, taken one step at a time, it is not difficult. Gowns with fitted bodices and full skirts are constructed in three stages. First, the bodice is assembled. Next, the skirt is assembled and attached to the bodice. Finally, the back closure and finishing details are applied; bridal gowns are also bustled at this time. Gowns with sheath or princess silhouettes often do not have waistlines. The bodices of these gowns are constructed in the same way, and the seams extend to the length of the skirt. The stage of assembling and attaching the skirt does not apply to gowns without waistline seams.

In the following pages, the assembly process has been broken down into construction steps that apply to a basic gown with or without an illusion, or sheer, neckline. While some of the steps may vary when you construct your gown, use this section as a guide to understanding the overall process of construction.

If you are using the zipper closure with buttons and loops, refer to the steps on pages 85 to 87 to be aware of the exceptions in the sequence of construction.

2) Assembling and attaching a skirt. The layers of the skirt and lining are assembled and attached separately. For additional volume, a separate cancan petticoat (page 122) may be worn with the gown.

3) Completing a gown. Finishing details include the back closure, hems, and any snaps or bustle buttons that are needed. Additional lace motifs or embellishments may be applied.

Assembling a Bodice

Once the test garment is fitted, the bodice can then be sewn with confidence. Although bodice styles vary, most require the same basic construction. A bodice with an illusion neckline is a variation of the basic style; the illusion area is assembled separately and inserted between the lower bodice and the lining. A fitted bodice may have several fabric layers, including an underlining, lining, outer fabric, and, perhaps, a lace overlay.

Lace may be added to the bodice in several ways (pages 103 to 105). Lightweight lace is usually basted to the right side of the outer fabric before the seams are sewn. Heavier laces, such as alençon, are cut to the contour of the bodice after the side seams are stitched, or applied in individual motifs.

To avoid overhandling, complete as much of the bodice as possible before attaching the skirt. This includes applying lace, sequins, and beads.

Illusion neckline is a popular variation for a fitted bodice. The illusion area may be made from any sheer fabric or from illusion net. For the illusion area of this garment, sheer fabric is used as the outer fabric and net as the lining.

How to Assemble a Fitted Bodice

1) Attach the boning (page 60), if specified on the pattern. Baste underlining to bodice pieces, *wrong* sides together, ½" (1.3 cm) from raw edges.

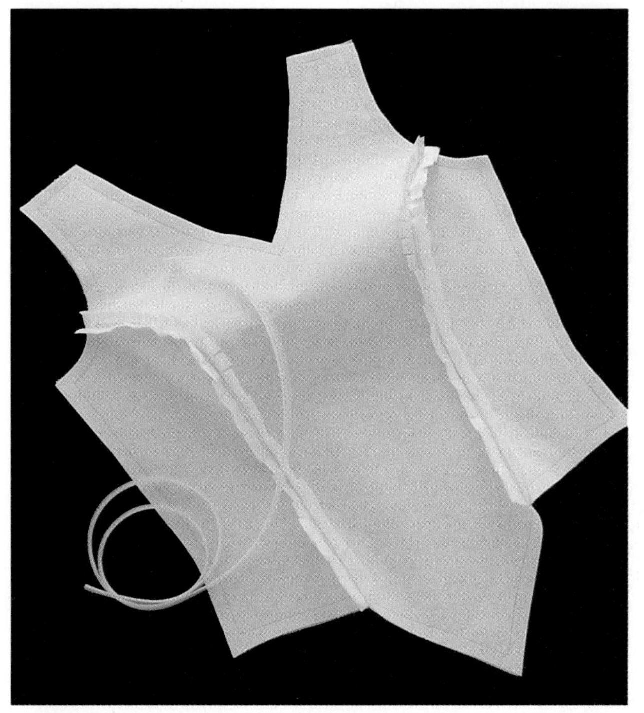

2) Stitch and press any princess seams or darts. Apply horsehair braid to princess seams (page 61), if desired.

(Continued on next page)

3) Stitch and press side seams. Pin or baste shoulder seams. Check the fit.

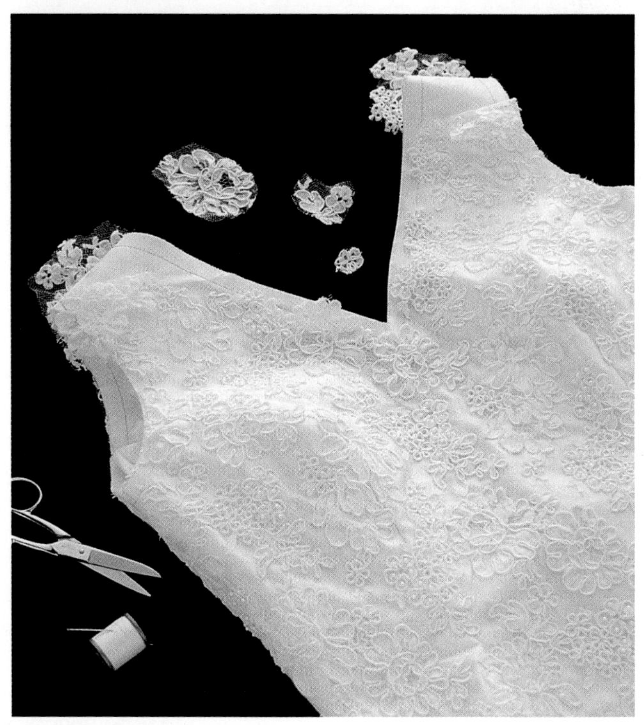

4) Cut and apply alençon lace to entire bodice and stitch shoulder seams as on pages 103 and 104, steps 1 to 9. Or stitch shoulder seams and cut and apply lace appliqués as on page 105, steps 1 to 3.

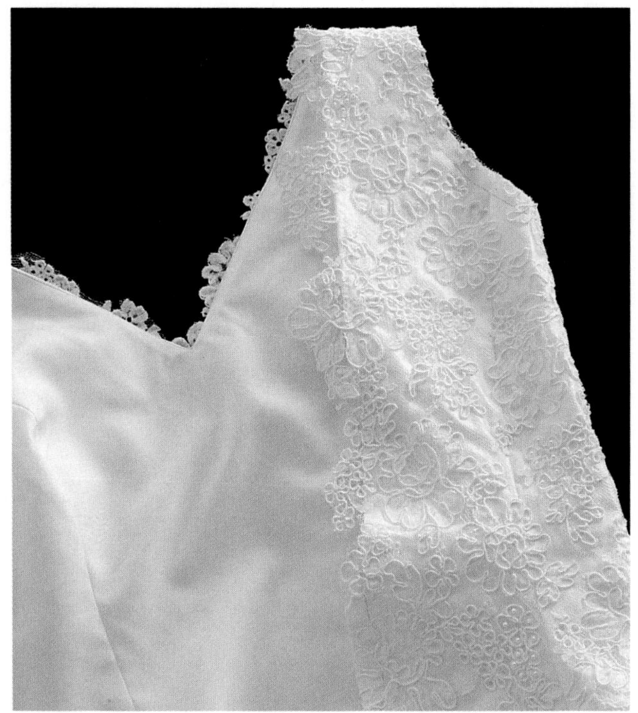

5) Assemble lining, and stitch to garment at neckline, right sides together, inserting pearl edging or piping (pages 64 and 65), if desired; if back has deep V neck, stitch to center back seamline. Stay the upper edge of a strapless gown (page 56). Trim and clip seam allowances; turn and press. Understitch seam (page 57).

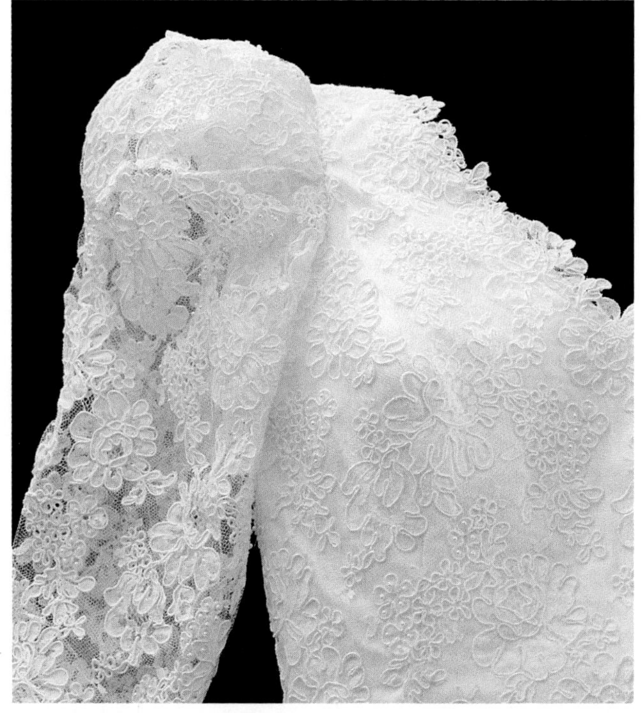

6) Baste lining to garment at armholes. Stitch sleeve seams, and set in sleeves. Apply sleeve headings, if desired (page 76). Finish neckline with lace, or add trim; leave ends free, if necessary, for back closure.

How to Assemble a Fitted Bodice with an Illusion Neckline

1) Follow steps 1 to 4 on pages 43 and 44, using lower bodice pieces.

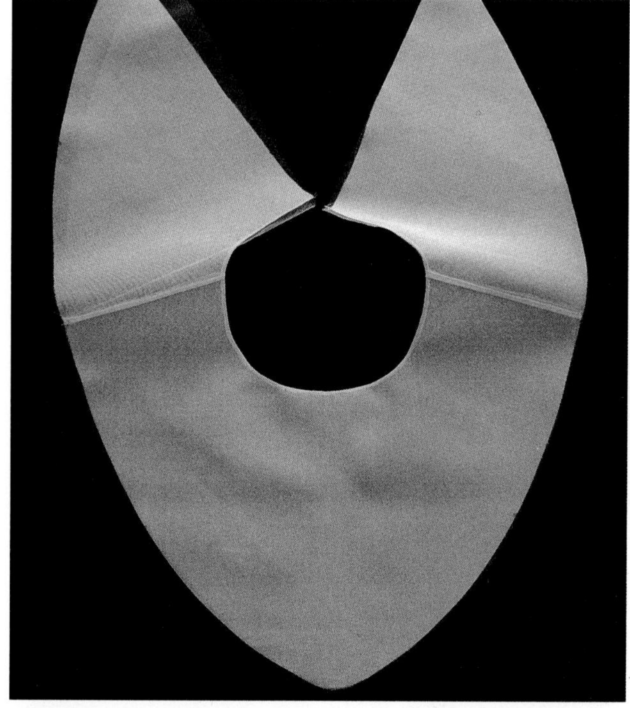

2) Stitch the shoulder seams of sheer upper bodice and lining, using double-stitched method (page 54). Stitch lining to upper bodice at neckline in a hairline seam (page 55). Turn right side out.

3) Press in center back seam allowances on upper bodice and upper bodice lining. Machine-baste upper bodice section to lower bodice, right sides together, a scant ⅝" (1.5 cm) from raw edges.

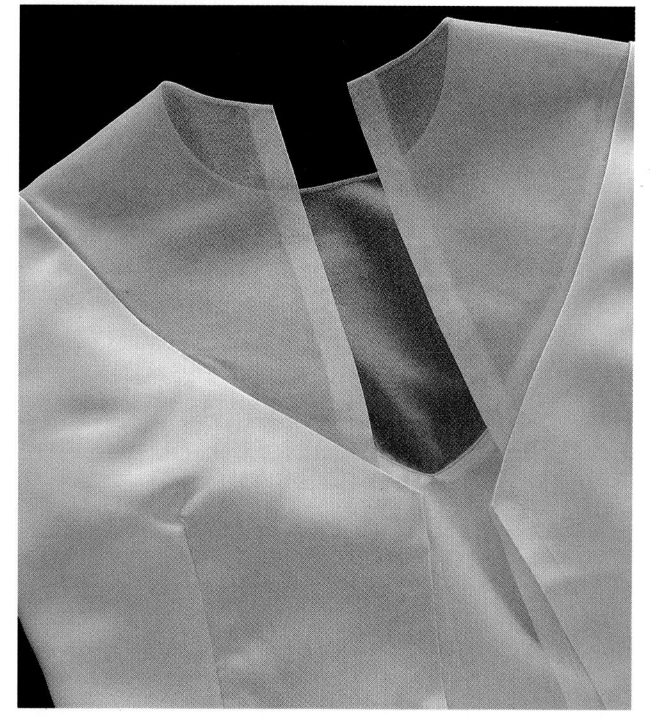

4) Assemble lower bodice lining; stitch to lower bodice, with upper bodice between layers. Trim and clip seam allowances; turn right side out, and understitch seam. Stitch sleeve seams, and set in sleeves; apply headings, if desired (page 76). Apply button and loop back closure to illusion (page 89). Add lace or trim, if desired.

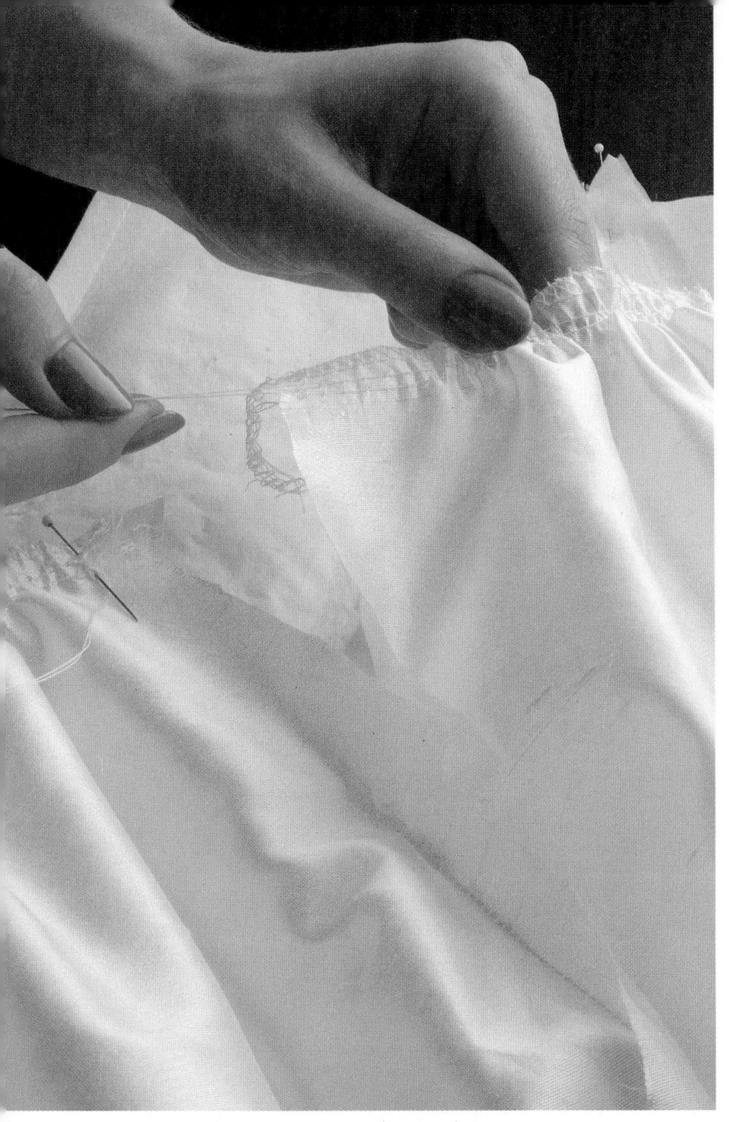

Skirt is pinned to the bodice, then gathered to fit.

Assembling & Attaching a Skirt

Lining eliminates the need for a slip or, when used with a cancan petticoat, it prevents the skirt fabric from catching on the cancan net. If the lining is cut the same as the skirt, assemble it separately and pleat it to fit the bodice, to reduce bulk at the waist. Many patterns include pattern pieces for an A-line skirt lining. The skirt lining is usually attached with the right side against the skirt. This prevents the seam allowances of the lining from showing through and gives a neater finish if the lining is exposed when the gown is worn.

Skirts with attached trains often have a floor-length lining that does not extend into the train. This style is assembled like a regular skirt with lining. Some skirts have one or more top layers of sheer fabric over a taffeta or lightweight satin underskirt. The seam allowances of the sheer overlay are hemmed at the center back opening; this allows the zipper to be stitched to the underskirt only. Tulle skirts usually have several layers of tulle. For ease in handling, all the tulle layers are sewn as one at the waistline seam; gather the layers by zigzagging over a cord (page 125).

How to Make and Attach a Skirt

1) Stitch skirt seams. Stitch two rows of gathering threads at upper edge of skirt; edge-finish upper edge of ravel-prone fabric. Stitch lining seams; if a zipper will be applied at center back seam, stitch lining seam to 1" (2.5 cm) below zipper opening.

How to Make and Attach a Skirt with an Overlay

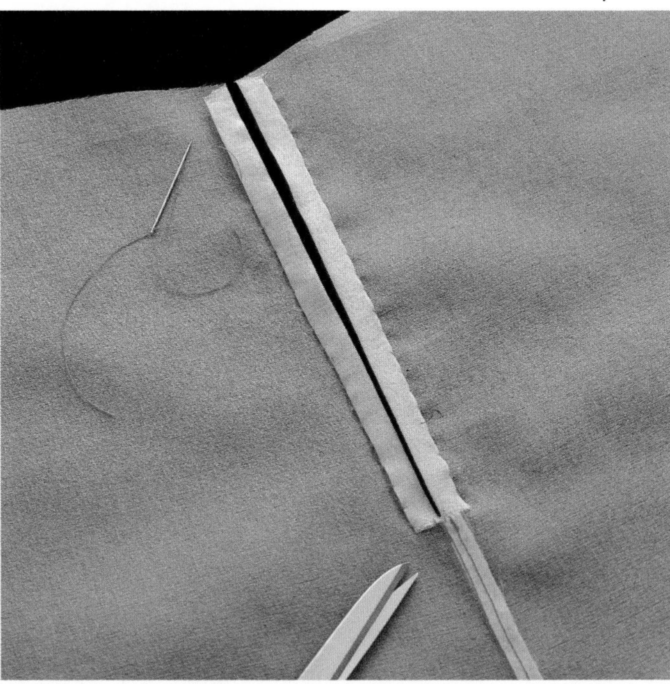

1) Stitch skirt overlay seams; clip seam at center back opening, and press under seam allowances above the seam. For organza or chiffon, fold a narrow hem, and slipstitch; tulle may be cut along pressed edge.

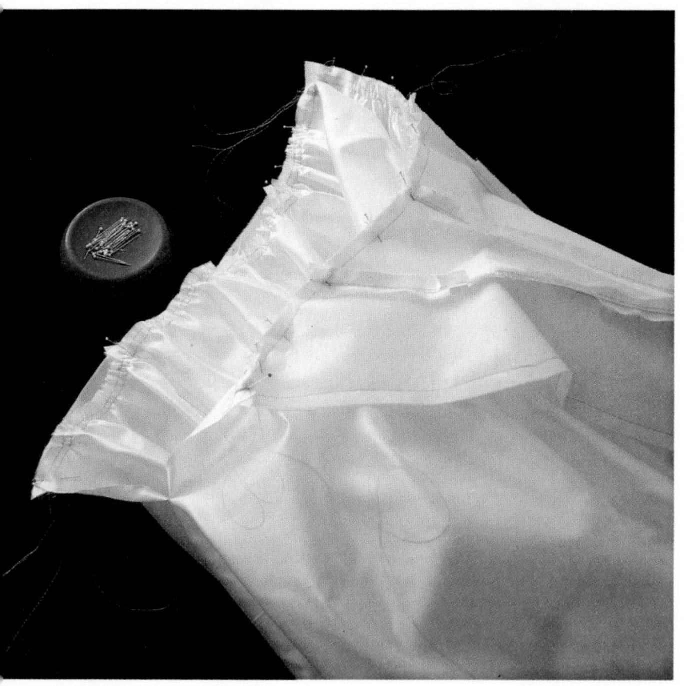

2) Pin skirt to bodice, right sides together, matching pattern markings and keeping bodice lining free. Gather skirt to fit the bodice; baste.

3) Pin skirt lining, wrong side up, over skirt; match pattern markings. At the center back, fold back the lining seam allowance 1/8" (3 mm) beyond seamline; if a lapped zipper will extend into skirt, fold left side of skirt lining 5/8" (1.5 cm) beyond seamline. Pleat lining to fit; stitch. Stay seam (page 56).

2) Stitch rows of gathering threads at upper edge of the skirt overlay. Pin overlay to bodice, right sides together, matching pattern markings and keeping bodice lining free; align hemmed edges of center back opening on skirt with center back seamlines of bodice.

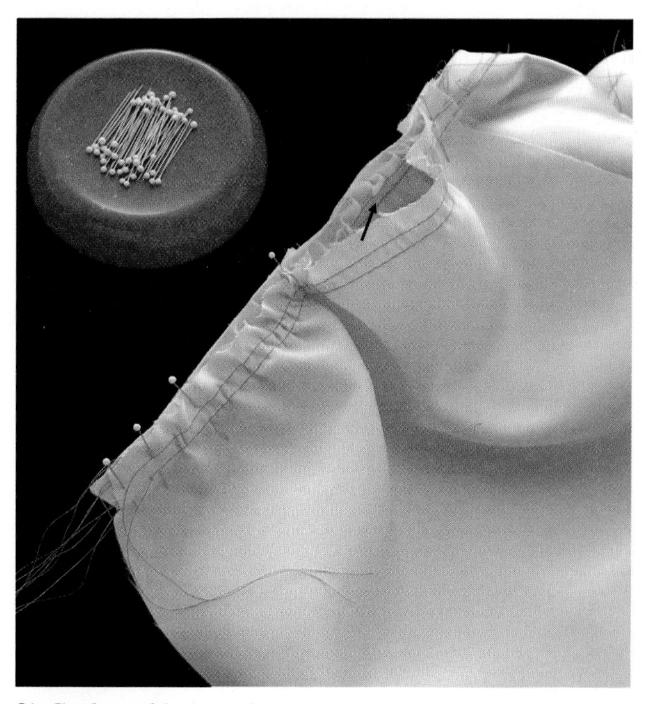

3) Gather skirt overlay to fit the bodice, and baste in place (arrow). Make and attach the underskirt, following steps 1 to 3, above.

Completed gown is stored with the bodice and sleeves stuffed with tissue paper. To prevent wrinkling, store a bridal gown with the train hanging from a separate hanger.

Completing a Gown

Lapped and invisible zippers are often used for back closures of gowns, with ready-made button looping inserted into the upper bodice of illusion necklines. These closures are usually one of the last steps in construction.

Skirt embellishments, such as lace appliqués, are applied after the skirt is hemmed. This allows them to be placed in the most flattering or prominent areas. Trims at the lower edge of the skirt are also applied after the skirt is hemmed. Additional lace appliqués or edgings may be added to conceal seams and zippers, or to finish the neckline.

Hang the gown on a padded hanger to reduce stress at the shoulder seams. For additional support, hang the garment from ribbon loops that are tacked to the side seams of the lining at the waistline. Allow sufficient room in the closet; any crushing will cause wrinkles. Preserve the shape of the bodice and sleeves by stuffing them with tissue paper.

How to Complete a Gown

1) Insert lapped or invisible zipper (pages 80 to 83).

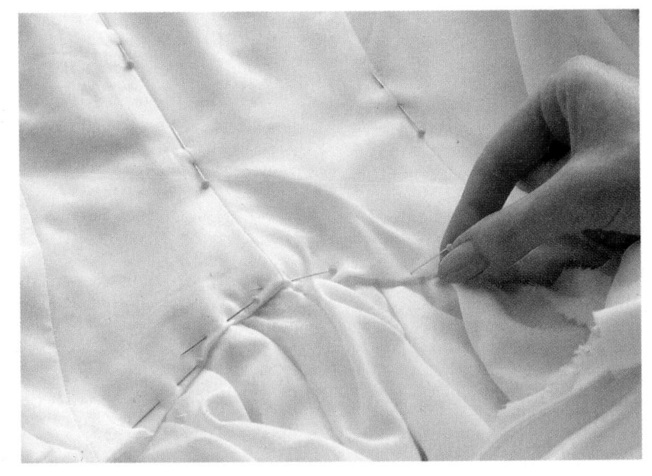

2) Pin garment and lining together at side seams or princess seams. Smooth lining to fit the bodice area; fold under seam allowance, and pin to waistline.

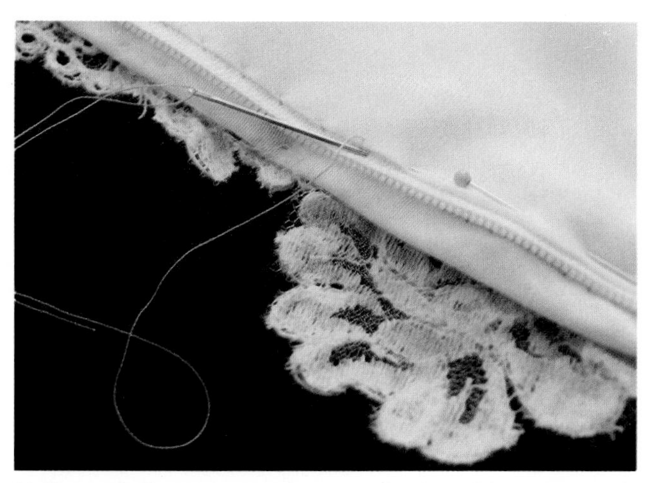

3) Smooth lining toward center back; fold under and pin lining to zipper tape; allow sufficient space for zipper to operate smoothly. Slipstitch lining in place.

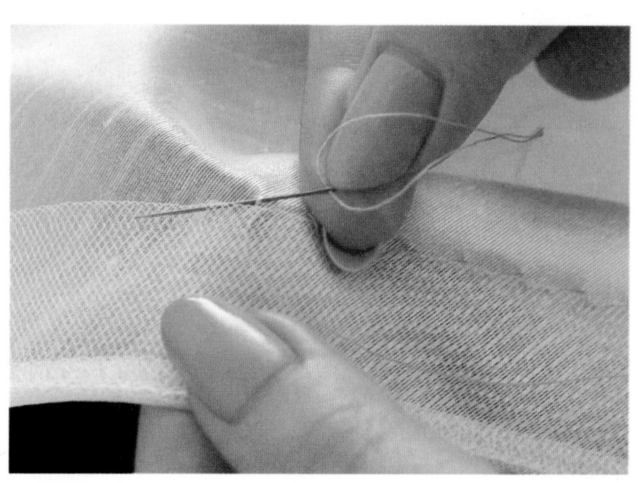

4) Allow the gown to hang for at least 24 hours. Hem lower edge (pages 91 to 93).

5) Add lace appliqués or other trims to the waistline or skirt, if desired; apply additional trims to neckline, if desired.

6) Bustle bridal gown with attached train (pages 95 to 99).

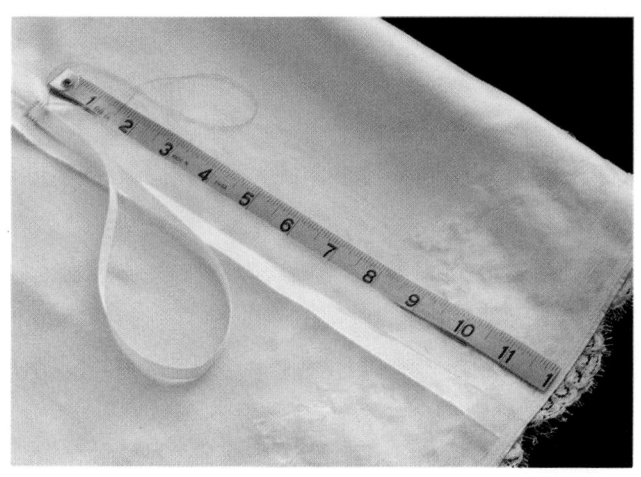

7) Attach loop of ribbon to wrong side of train, about 12" (30.5 cm) from end.

8) Attach loops of ribbon to side seams of the lining at waistline. Stuff gown with tissue paper. Hang gown; hang train from ribbon on separate hanger.

Specialized Sewing Techniques

Seams & Seam Finishes

Several types of seams are appropriate for sewing special-occasion garments. Choose the seam that works best for the fabric and the type of construction. Also take into consideration the quality and use of the garment and the amount of wear it will receive.

Make a variety of seams on fabric scraps to decide which methods you like best. You may find it helpful to use more than one type of seam within a single garment.

Stitching & Handling Tips

Always start with a new needle in the smallest size appropriate for the fabric; this minimizes permanent needle holes and helps to prevent skipped stitches. Change needles often when sewing large projects or sequined fabrics, which quickly dull needles.

Prevent puckered seams by holding the fabric taut as you sew. Hold the thread ends at the beginning of each seam; this prevents thread jams and keeps lightweight fabrics from being pushed down into the needle plate.

When stitching seams in lightweight fabrics, use a lightweight thread. Shortening the stitch length may improve the stitch quality. Prevent slippery fabrics from shifting by placing a layer of tissue paper under the seam; remove the tissue after stitching.

There are several ways to reduce the uneven feeding that often occurs when stitching velvets. Stitch in the direction of the nap whenever possible. Stop stitching every 2" to 3" (5 to 7.5 cm) with the needle down in the fabric, and raise the presser foot; this allows the fabric layers to relax. It is also helpful to decrease pressure on the presser foot, or to use an Even Feed® or roller foot. Additional pinning or hand basting may be necessary as well, especially on curved seams.

When sewing heavily sequined fabrics, remove the sequins from the seam allowances before stitching. For fabrics with scattered sequins that are secured with a three-prong stitch, you can stitch directly through the sequins; if the garment is unlined, you may want to bind the seam allowances (page 57) to prevent the sequins from irritating your skin.

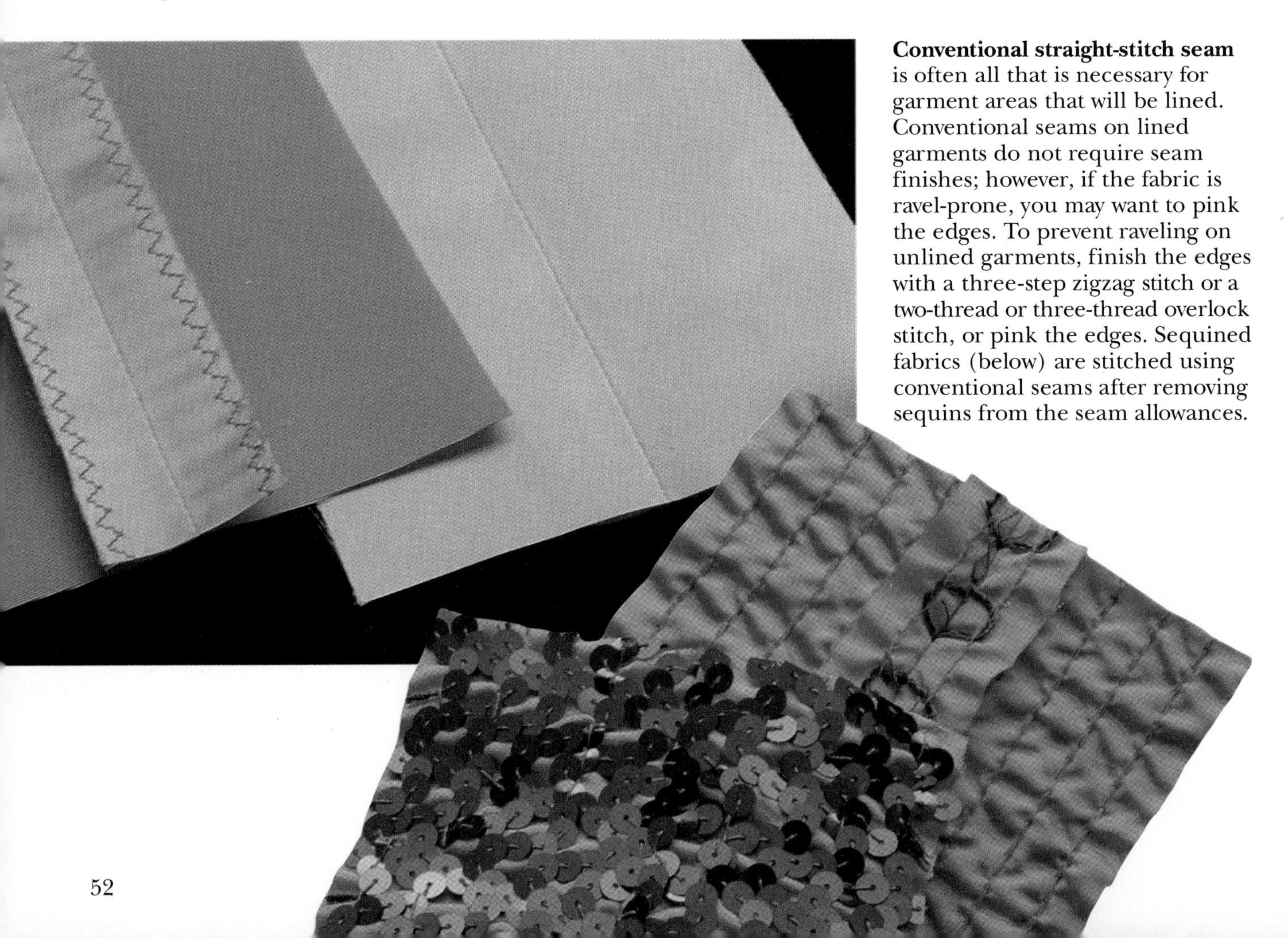

Conventional straight-stitch seam is often all that is necessary for garment areas that will be lined. Conventional seams on lined garments do not require seam finishes; however, if the fabric is ravel-prone, you may want to pink the edges. To prevent raveling on unlined garments, finish the edges with a three-step zigzag stitch or a two-thread or three-thread overlock stitch, or pink the edges. Sequined fabrics (below) are stitched using conventional seams after removing sequins from the seam allowances.

Double-stitched seam is a variation of the conventional straight-stitch seam. Faster than sewing a French seam, it is a suitable narrow seam on fabrics that do not ravel easily, such as net, organza, and lace.

Overlock seam is sewn on a serger, which easily handles thin, slippery fabrics without puckering them. Overlock seams are appropriate for quick seams on skirt linings, ruffles, and petticoats.

French seam is used for a quality finish on lightweight fabric. Because all the raw edges are enclosed, this seam is especially good for sheer and silky fabrics that ravel. French seams are used for straight seams and seams that need to be stabilized. Do not use French seams on curved seams, such as princess seams.

Hairline seam (left) is nearly invisible. This seam is for enclosed seams, such as those on collars and cuffs. The hairline seam is appropriate for sheer and silky fabrics.

How to Sew a Conventional Straight-stitch Seam

1) Stitch seam, right sides together; hold fabric taut to help prevent puckering. Press seam flat, then open.

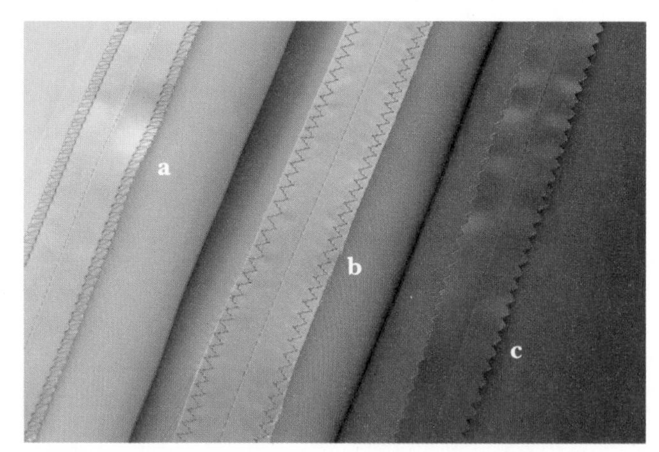

2) Finish seam, if desired, to prevent raveling. Use a three-thread or two-thread overlock stitch **(a)** or a three-step zigzag stitch **(b)**, or pink the edges **(c)**.

How to Sew a Seam on Sequined Fabrics

1) Secure the chainstitches on the wrong side of the fabric by pulling on the loop.

2) Remove the sequins from seam allowances by slipping them off the threads; set aside. Stitch over the threads to secure them.

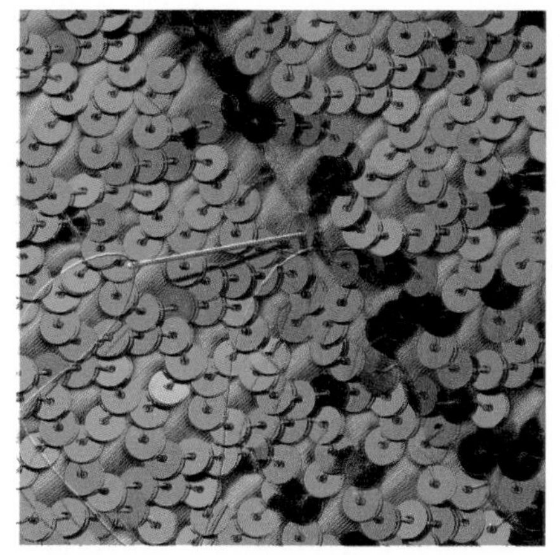

3) Stitch the seam, using a long stitch length; press open. At gaps between sequins, stitch reserved sequins in place.

How to Sew a Double-stitched Seam

1) Stitch conventional straight-stitch seam, above; stitch again 1⁄8" (3 mm) from previous stitching, within seam allowances.

2) Trim seam allowances close to stitching. Press the seam flat, then press to one side.

How to Sew an Overlock Seam

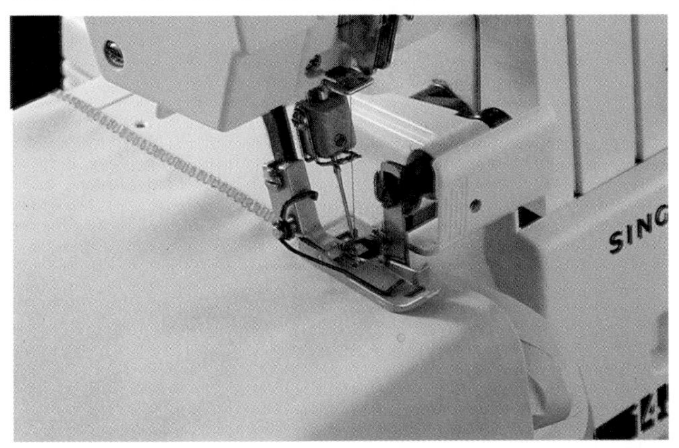

1) Stitch seam, right sides together, using balanced three-thread overlock stitch on serger and trimming seam allowances with serger blades.

2) Press seam flat, then press to one side; prevent imprinting the seam edges on the right side by inserting strip of paper under seam allowances.

How to Sew a French Seam

1) Stitch seam, *wrong* sides together, using 3/8" (1 cm) seam allowances and short straight stitches. Press seam flat.

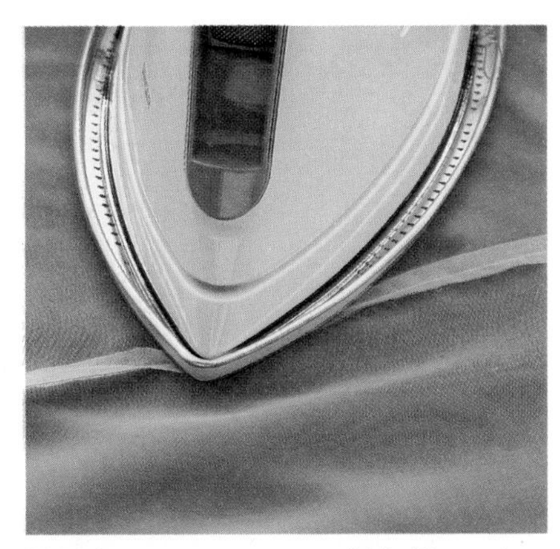

2) Trim seam to scant 1/4" (6 mm). Press seam open.

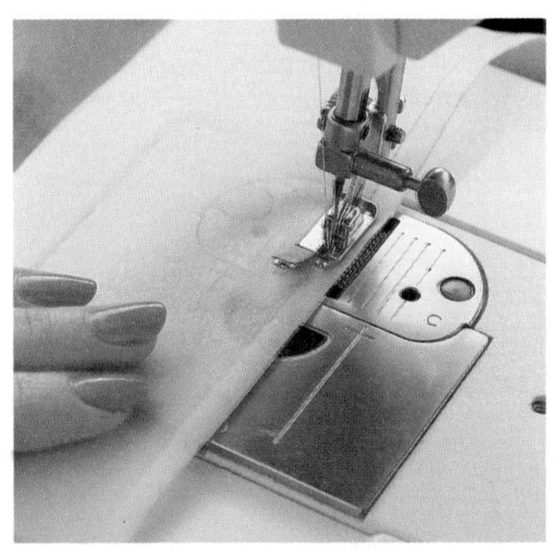

3) Fold fabric, right sides together; press seam edge. Stitch 1/4" (6 mm) seam; press to one side.

How to Sew a Hairline Seam

1) Stitch 5/8" (1.5 cm) seam, right sides together, using short straight stitches. Stitch seam again with a narrow zigzag stitch, so the needle pierces fabric close to seamline.

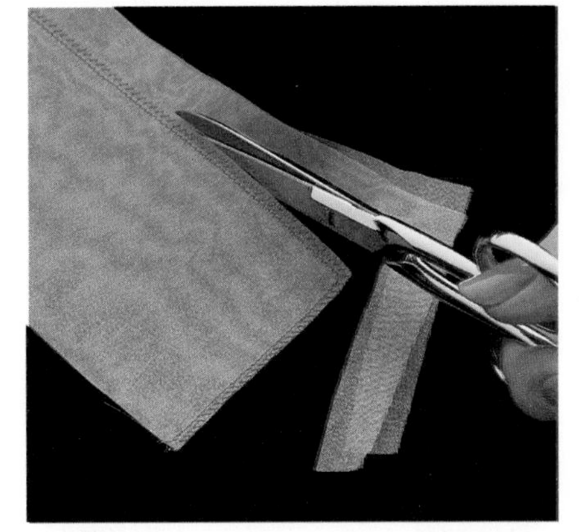

2) Trim seam allowances close to zigzag stitches. Use small, sharp scissors for clean, neat edges.

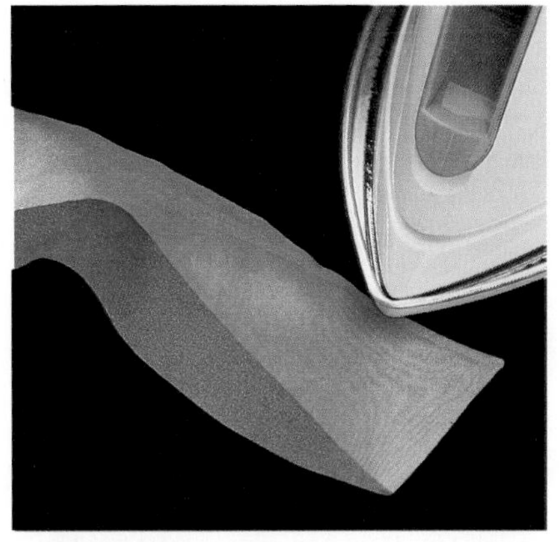

3) Turn right side out; press with tip of iron to avoid imprinting the seam edges on right side.

Stayed, Understitched & Bound Seams

Specialty seam techniques are often used at waistlines, necklines, and armholes, either to strengthen seams, make them more comfortable, or make them neater in appearance. These techniques include understitching, staying, and binding.

Stayed seams are reinforced by stitching narrow twill tape or ribbon over the seams. This prevents the seams from stretching and reinforces seams on fragile fabrics that will receive stress. Staying is usually used for the waistline seam, the upper edge of strapless and off-the-shoulder bodices, and the shoulder seams of garments made from fragile or loosely woven fabrics.

Understitching keeps the linings and facings from rolling to the right side of the garment. The seam allowances are finger-pressed toward the lining or facing; then the layers are stitched together.

Binding encases a seam edge; for a bound edge that does not add bulk, use a sheer tricot bias binding. It is used for a neater edge finish at the neckline of a sheer garment or the armholes of a lined garment, and as a seam finish for fabrics that may be irritating to the skin. When binding the underarm area of an armhole, trim the seam allowances to 1/4" (6 mm) between the notches; do not trim the seam allowances in the sleeve cap area.

Sewing Stayed Seams

Stay seam by positioning twill tape or ribbon over seamline; stitch just inside stitched seam. At waistline, stitch tape on bodice side of seam allowance; at upper edge of strapless gown, stitch tape on lining side of seam allowance.

Sewing Understitched Seams

Understitch seam by trimming and clipping the seam allowances, then finger-pressing them toward lining or facing. Stitch on right side of lining or facing, close to seamline. Upper edge of strapless gown may be stayed before it is understitched.

Sewing Bound Seams

Bind seam allowances by folding tricot bias binding in half lengthwise and encasing raw edges. Stretch strip slightly as you sew, so strip folds over edge; stitch with straight stitch or medium-width zigzag stitch.

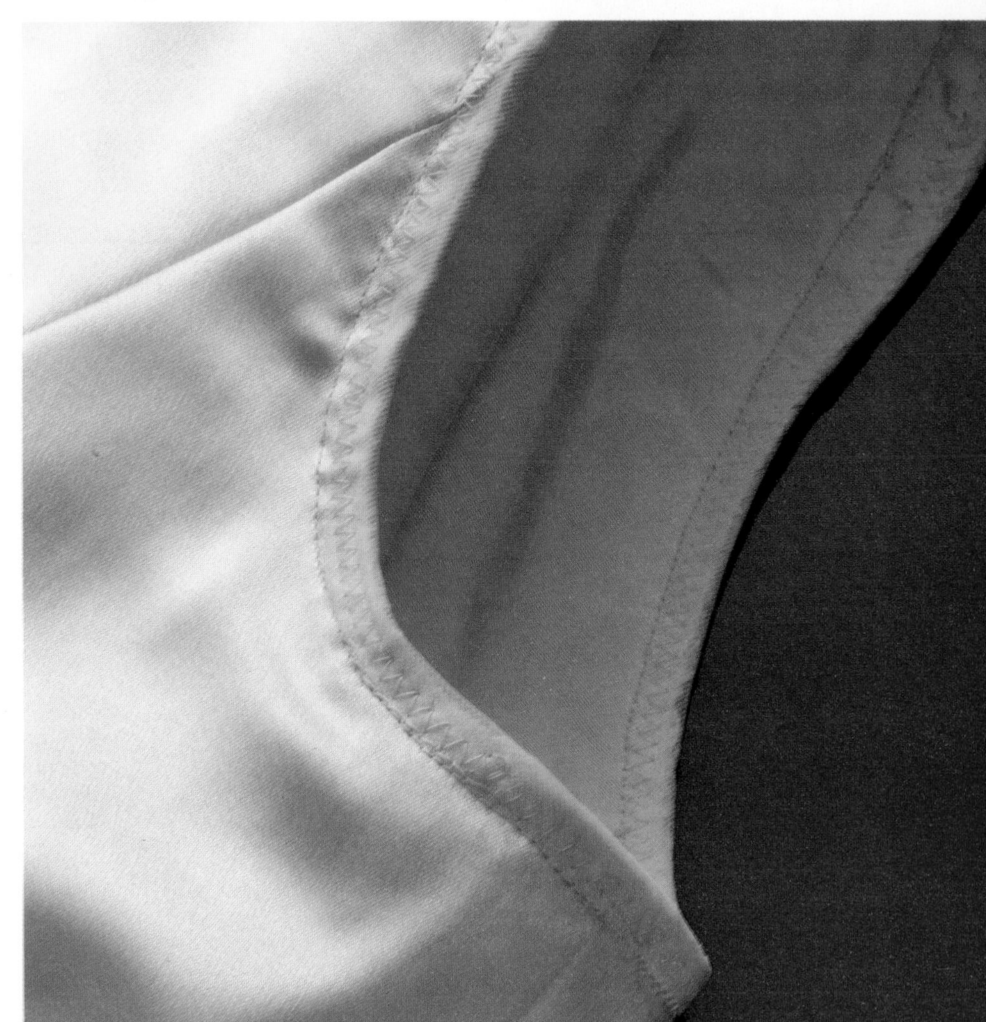

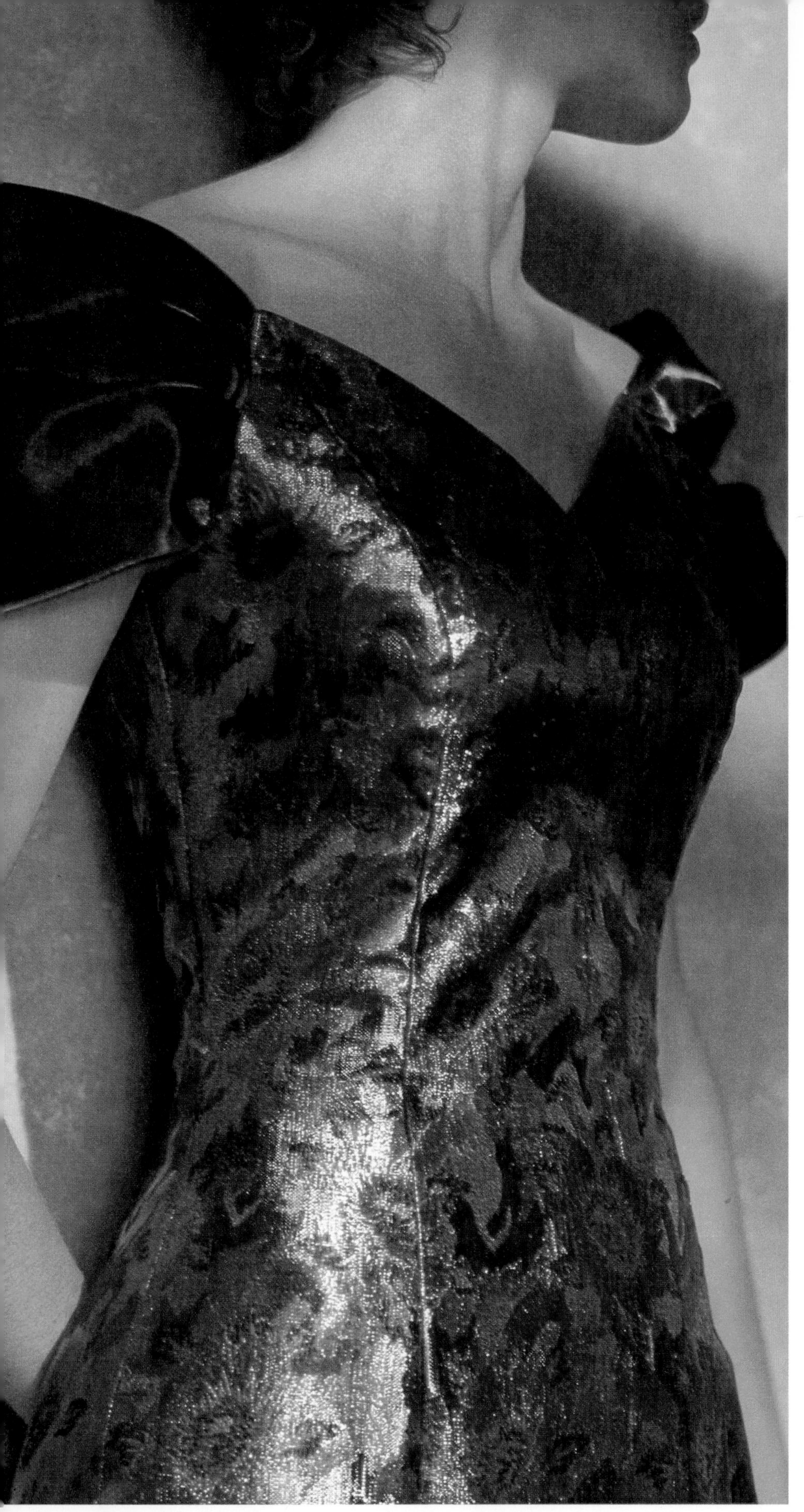

Boning provides smooth, comfortable support in the bodice of a close-fitting off-the-shoulder or strapless dress.

Shaping the Bodice

There are several ways to shape a bodice with the use of boning, horsehair braid, or padded bra cups. The shaping method you select depends on the style of the garment and whether you want firm support, subtle shaping, or additional bustline fullness.

Boning

Boning provides a smooth fit in the bodice of a close-fitting off-the-shoulder or strapless gown. It also prevents the garment from shifting when it is worn. If the pattern calls for boning, do not omit it. The boning is necessary for fitting the garment properly, regardless of the bust size.

Boning has a built-in curve and is applied so the ends of the boning will curve toward your body when the garment is worn. Boning can be applied to underlined or lined garments, and is positioned at vertical seams or placement lines.

When boning is used at seamlines, it is applied to the outer fabric. For a garment with underlining, it is applied after the bodice seams are stitched.

When boning is positioned at the placement lines provided on the pattern, it is applied to the underlining before the outer fabric and the underlining are basted together. For a lined garment without underlining, the boning is applied at the placement lines on the wrong side of the lining.

There are various types of boning, offering varying degrees of stiffness. Plastic boning is covered with woven fabric or nonwoven interfacing. Another type of boning is made from polypropylene filaments that are interwoven with polyester. Any of these types of boning can be positioned either at seamlines or placement lines.

Horsehair Braid

Horsehair braid can be used for the subtle shaping of princess seams, creating smooth seams with a natural curve. The horsehair braid is applied to the front princess seams of the outer fabric, from the seamline at the armhole or shoulder to the waistline. For a garment with underlining, the horsehair braid is applied after the bodice seams are stitched.

Bridal Bra Cups

If full shaping is desired, padded bra cups can be added to a bodice. Bra cups may be used in addition to boning or horsehair braid.

Bridal bra cups, available in various cup sizes, are padded for a smooth, natural contour. When checking the fit of the test garment (page 20), pin the bra cups to either the muslin or your undergarments.

Bra cups are inserted so they are concealed by the lining. Attach the bra cups to the underlining before the lining is secured at the waistline and back closure.

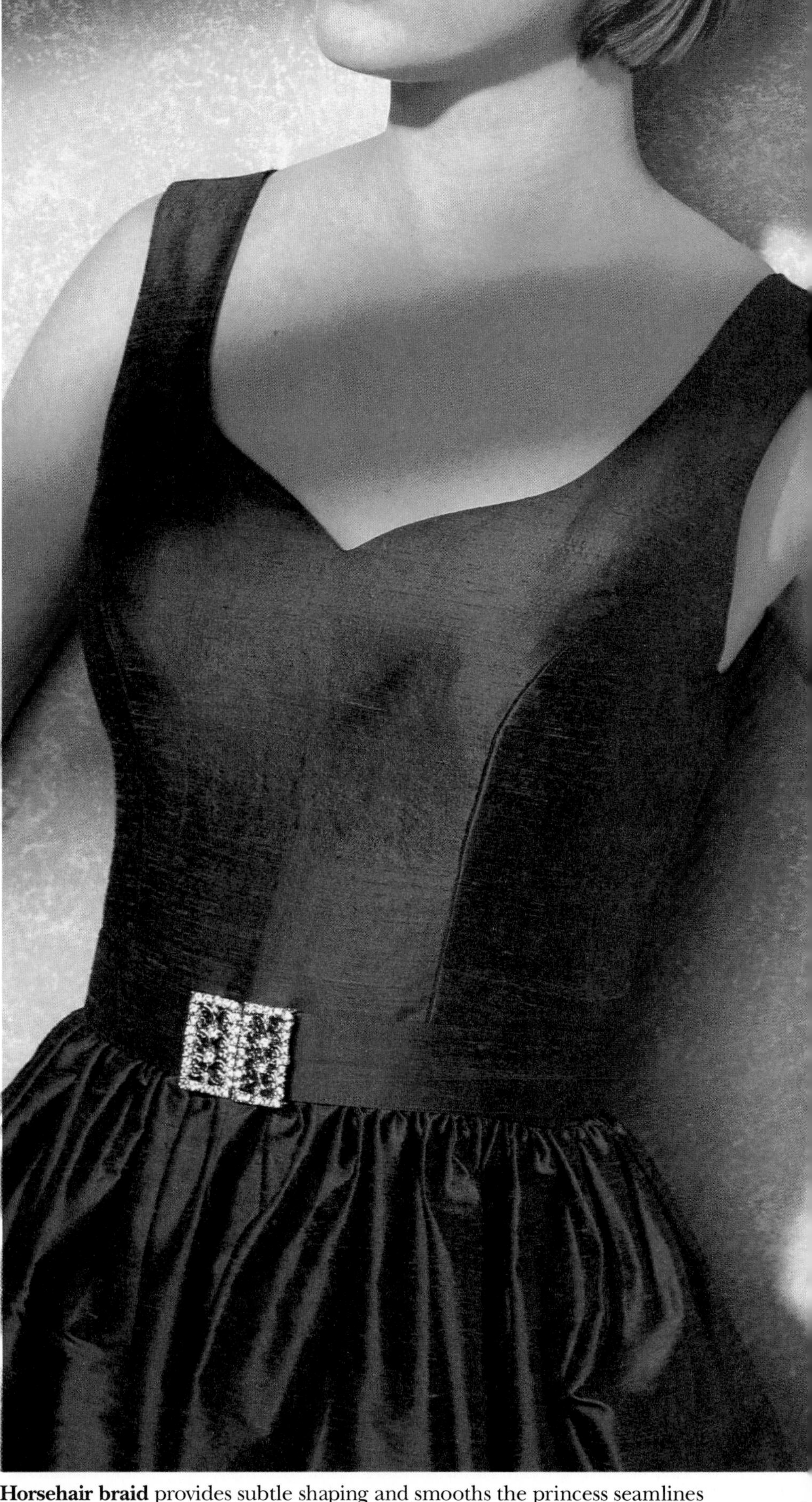

Horsehair braid provides subtle shaping and smooths the princess seamlines of a dress.

How to Apply Polypropylene Boning

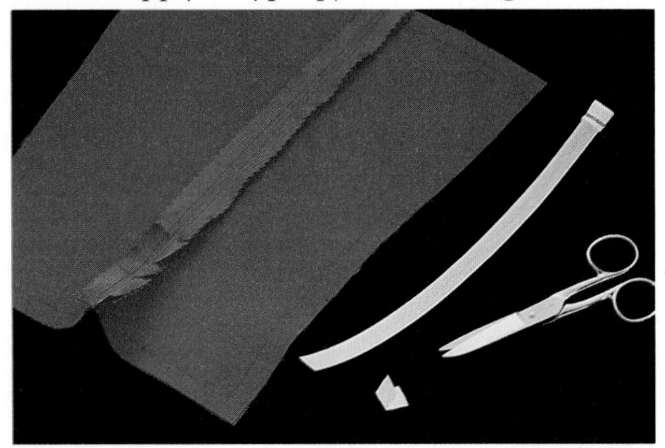

1) Cut boning to length of placement line where it will be applied; boning does not extend into seam allowances. Cut 1" (2.5 cm) piece of ½" (1.3 cm) twill tape for each end of boning. Fold twill tape in half, and place over end. Stitch through all layers about ⅜" (1 cm) from end of boning.

2) Place boning in position, so ends will curve toward the body. Machine-stitch along edges of boning, using general-purpose presser foot; if applying boning to seam allowances of garment, stitch to seam allowances only.

How to Apply Covered Plastic Boning

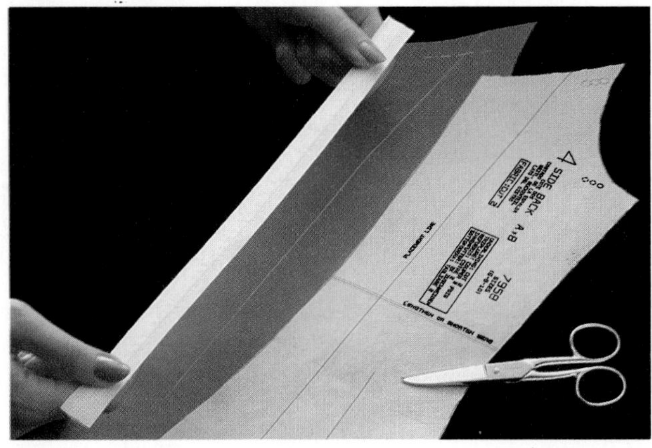

1) Cut boning 1" (2.5 cm) longer than placement line where boning will be applied; boning does not extend into seam allowances.

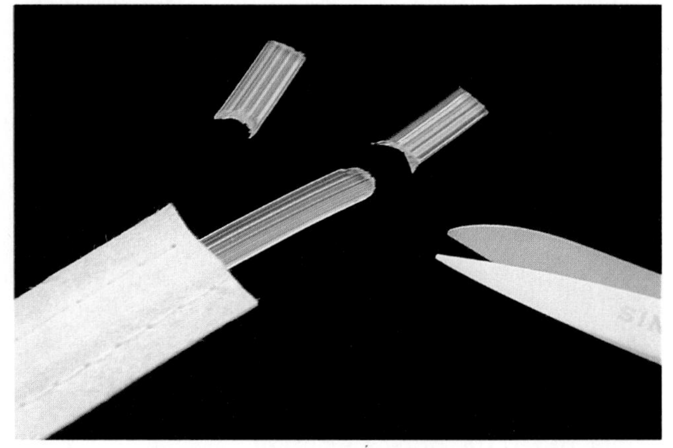

2) Push end of the boning strip out of the covering. Trim away ½" (1.3 cm) of the boning, rounding any sharp corners. Repeat for other end.

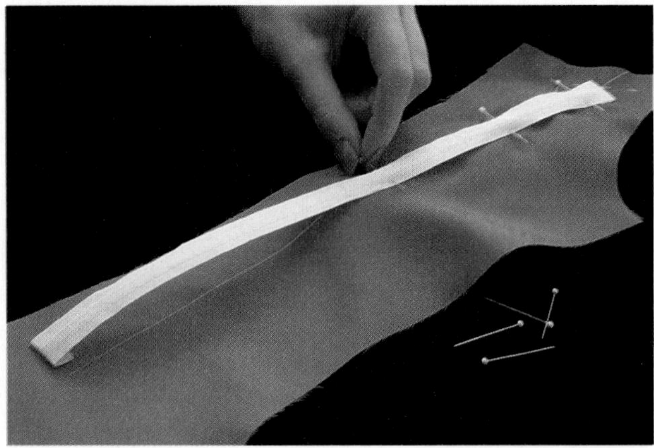

3) Fold ends of covering to underside of the boning. Place boning over marked lines or seam, so ends will curve toward the body.

4) Machine-stitch along edges of covering, using general-purpose presser foot; if applying the boning to seam allowances of garment, stitch to seam allowances only.

How to Apply Horsehair Braid

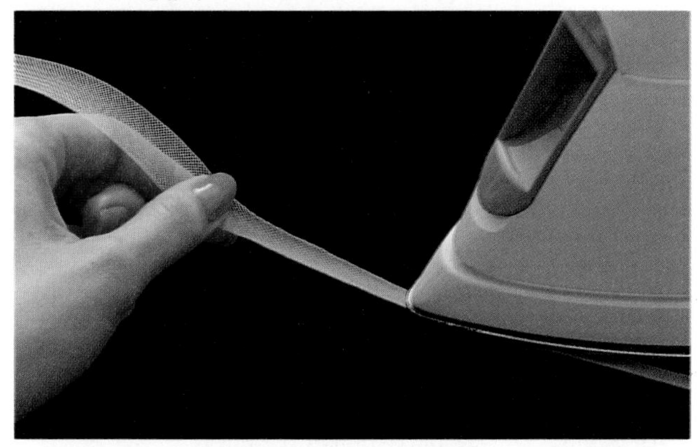

1) Stretch a length of ½" (1.3 cm) horsehair braid; steam press. Braid will shrink in width. Cut a length slightly longer than seamline where horsehair braid will be applied.

2) Cut a length of ½" (1.3 cm) horsehair braid to same length as narrow strip from step 1. Center the narrow strip over wide strip; stitch strips together through center.

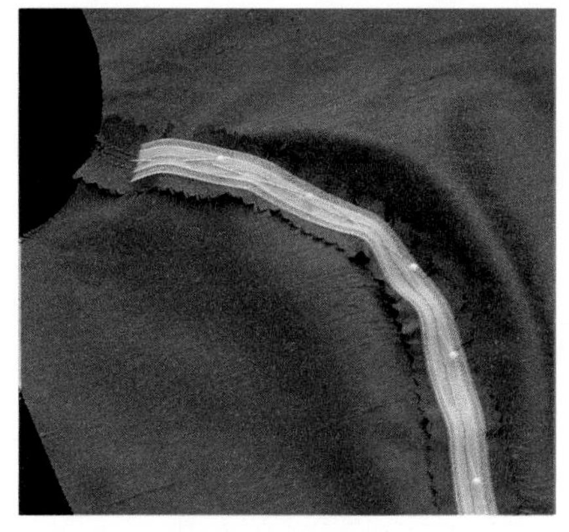

3) Pin the stitched braid to the seam allowance of princess seam, curving braid to contour the seam; the braid should start at the waistline seam and extend to armhole or shoulder seam. Trim braid at seamlines.

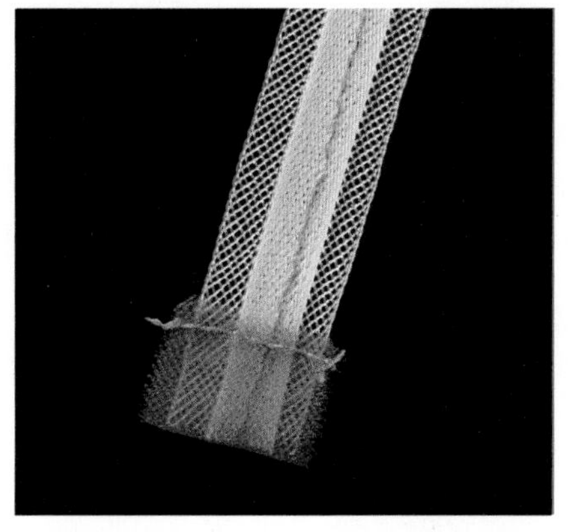

4) Fold and stitch 1" (2.5 cm) strip of tricot bias binding over ends of horsehair braid.

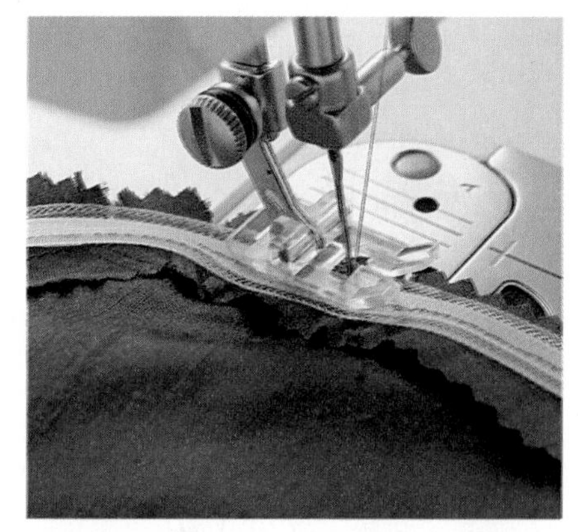

5) Fold garment to one side at seam allowance; stitch tape along one edge, stitching through braid and seam allowance. Repeat at opposite side of braid.

How to Apply Bridal Bra Cups

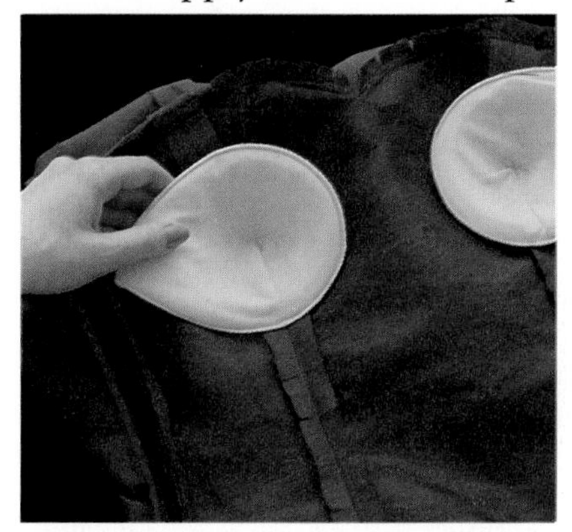

1) Position bridal bra cups, with darts on bottom, between bodice and lining. Try on garment; adjust position, pinning from the right side of the bodice.

2) Pin bra cups from the wrong of the bodice; remove outer pins. Try on the garment, and recheck the position of the bra cups for even placement.

3) Hand-stitch bra cups to seam allowances at upper and lower edges. If bodice is underlined, also secure at the tapered ends, catching the underlining only.

Pearl edging and satin piping are finishes that add emphasis to a neckline. Both trims are inserted into the seam.

Lace edging highlights a bridesmaid's dress or mother-of-the-bride's dress.

Neckline Finishes

There are a number of neckline finishes that can add distinctive detailing to a garment. Some, such as piping and French binding, are incorporated during the construction process, while others, such as sequined appliqués, are added after the garment is completed.

Pearl Edging & Piping

Pearl edging and piping add definition to necklines and are easy to insert into the neckline seam. Pearl edging, attached to a tricot strip, does not add bulk to seam allowances. Satin piping is available in white, black, and ivory. Or make your own piping, using bias fabric strips and narrow cording.

Lace Edgings

Narrow lace edgings, suitable for neckline trims, are available in a variety of styles and widths, or they may be cut from galloon laces. Lace edging is usually attached after the garment is completed, because it is then easier to determine the placement. For an attractive effect, many laces can be extended beyond the neckline.

Beaded appliqués and rhinestone trims add sparkle to a garment with simple styling.

Glittering Trims

Glittering trims, such as beaded and sequined appliqués and rhinestone trims, make even simple garments look glamorous. When selecting trims, make sure they are flexible enough to ease smoothly around the curve of the neckline. It is recommended that these trims be removed when the garment is cleaned; for this reason, hand-stitch the trims onto the completed garment.

French Binding

French binding is often used to finish the neckline edge of a sheer garment, because it eliminates the need for a facing. Made from a folded strip of bias fabric, it conceals and strengthens the raw edge. Binding is generally applied at the neckline after the back closure is inserted. If the binding is applied to a lined garment, do not stitch the neckline seam, and treat the garment and lining as one layer of fabric.

For a binding that lies flat and smooth, cut the fabric strips on the true bias. The instructions on page 67 are for a ¼" (6 mm) binding.

French binding eliminates the need for a facing on the neckline of a sheer garment.

How to Apply Pearl Edging

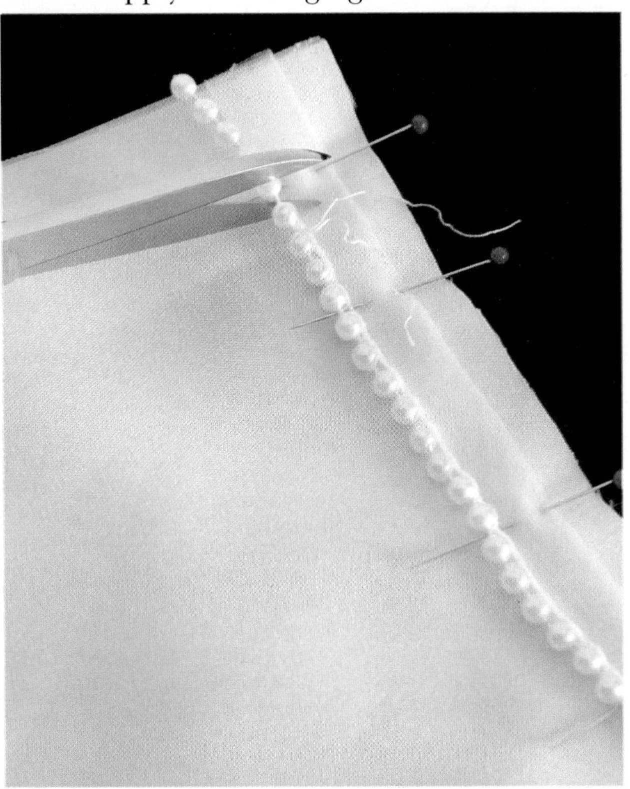

1) Pin pearl edging to right side of garment, with edge of pearls next to seamline. At ends, remove stitching in tricot tape and cut pearls at back seamline.

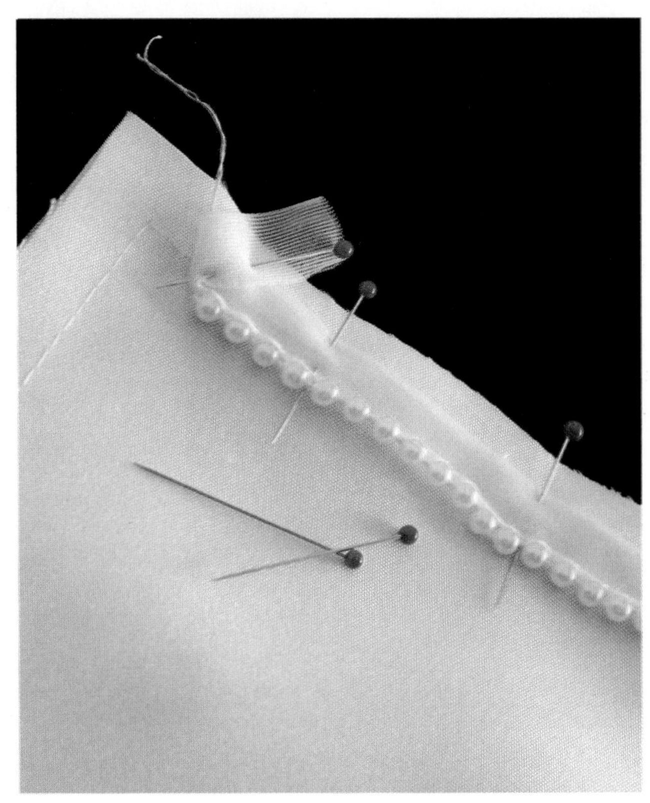

2) Knot the thread ends. Fold ends of the tricot tape into neckline seam allowance.

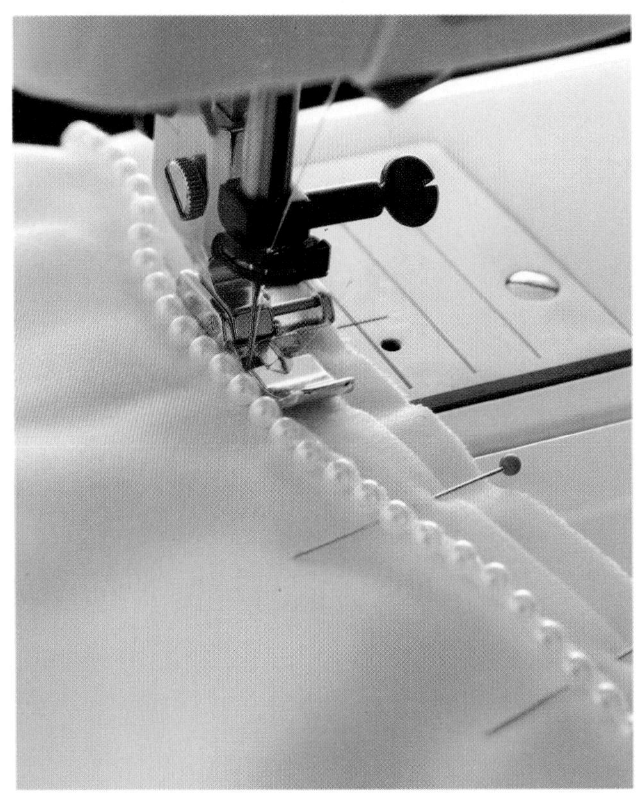

3) Stitch a scant 5⁄8" (1.5 cm) from raw edges, using a zipper foot.

4) Attach lining at the neckline, stitching on the 5⁄8" (1.5 cm) seamline.

How to Apply Piping

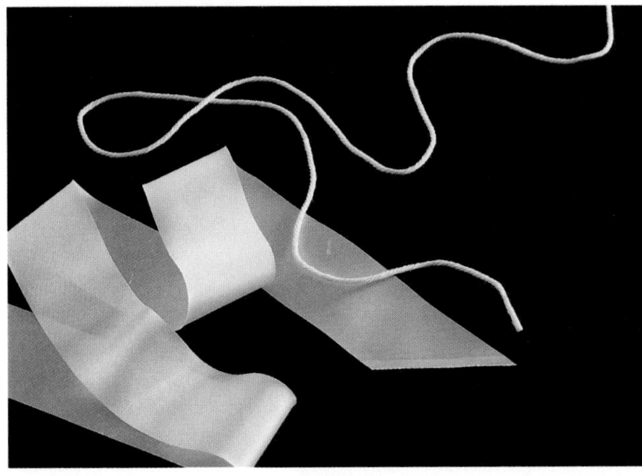

1) Cut 2" (5 cm) fabric strip on true bias, with cut length of strip equal to distance around neckline plus extra for finishing ends.

2) Center cording on wrong side of fabric strip. Fold fabric strip in half lengthwise, wrong sides together, enclosing cording. Stitch close to cord, using zipper foot. Trim seam allowances to match those of garment.

3) Pin piping to right side of garment, raw edges even. Clip piping seam allowances at corners and curves so they lie flat; at inside corner, also clip garment seam allowance.

4) Taper the piping into neckline seam allowances at back opening so cording will not extend into back seam allowances. Seam allowances at back opening are 1" (2.5 cm).

5) Stitch a scant ⅝" (1.5 cm) from raw edges. Remove stitching in piping at ends; trim cord.

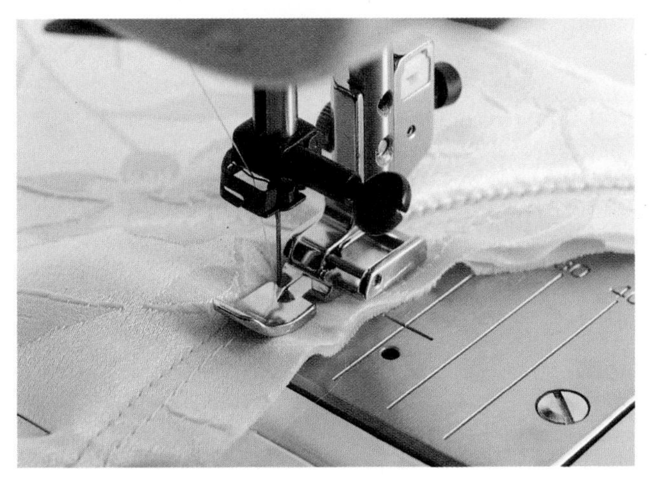

6) Attach lining at the neckline, stitching on the ⅝" (1.5 cm) seamline.

How to Apply Lace Edging

1) Pin lace edging around neckline, extending edge of lace beyond neck edge, if desired; some laces may need to be clipped so they lie smooth.

2) Hand-stitch the lace edging in place, using short running stitches; conceal stitches in design of lace.

How to Apply Rhinestone Trims

Hand-stitch over the base of the trim, working from the right side of the garment; take one stitch between rhinestones, or space stitches at 1/4" to 3/8" (6 mm to 1 cm) intervals.

How to Apply Beaded or Sequined Trims

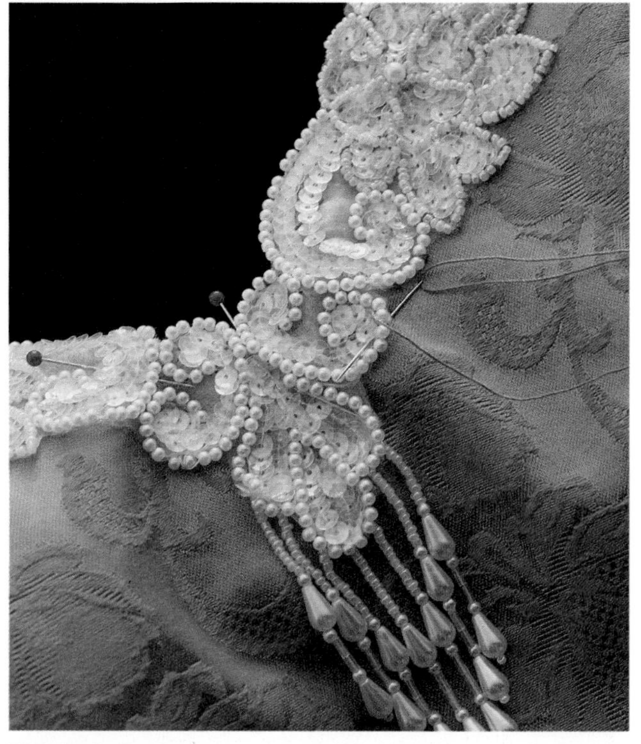

Hand-stitch trim to garment, with small stitches between beads or sequins. So trim will lie flat, avoid pulling stitches too tight.

How to Apply French Binding

1) Cut bias strips 1¾" (4.5 cm) wide by the length of edge to be bound plus extra for finishing ends. This makes ¼" (6 mm) finished binding.

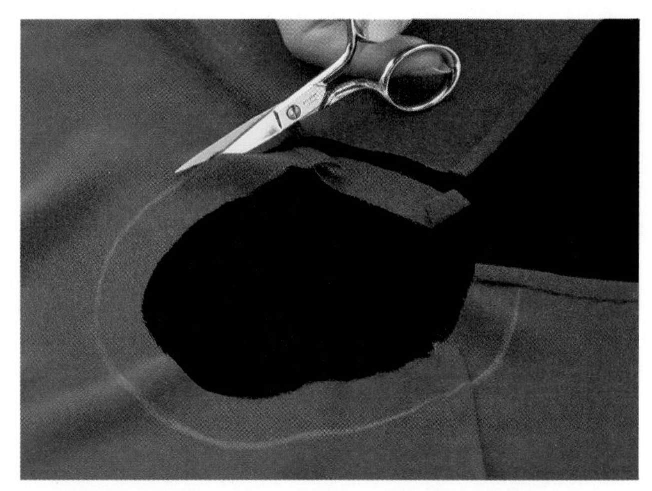

2) Mark seamline on garment edge; trim off entire seam allowance. Fold bias strip in half lengthwise, wrong sides together; press.

3) Pin binding to right side of garment, matching the raw edges and extending ends of binding ½" (1.3 cm) beyond opening. Stitch ¼" (6 mm) seam.

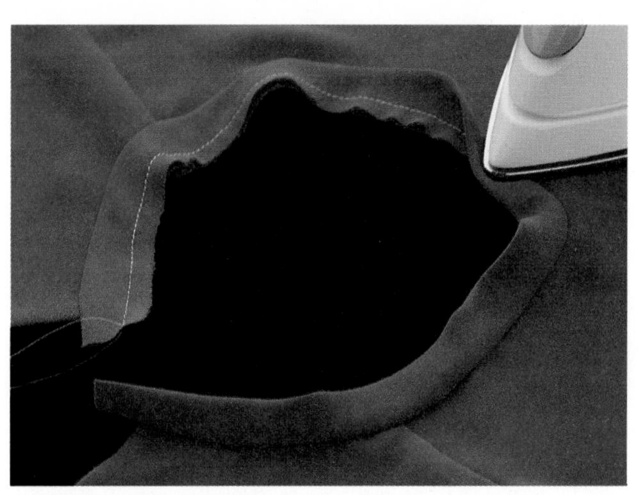

4) Press binding away from garment, with the seam allowances toward binding.

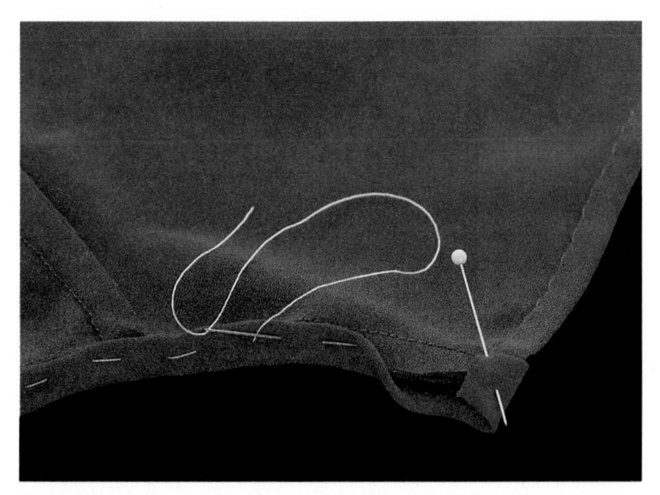

5) Fold ends of binding around seam allowances as shown; trim excess binding. Fold and press binding around neckline edge; hand-baste or pin.

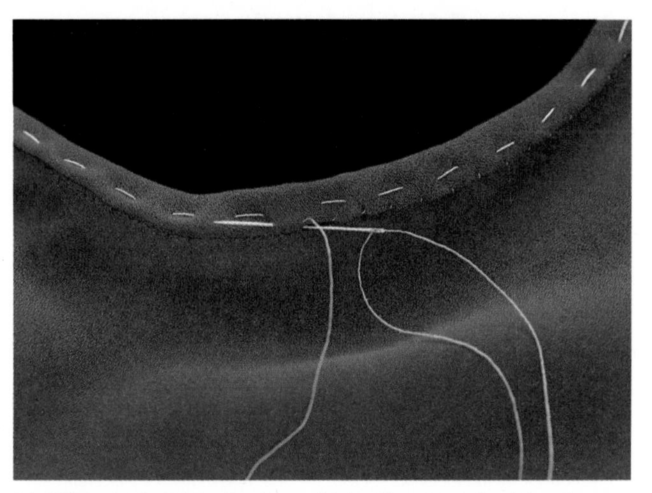

6) Slipstitch folded edge of binding just inside the seamline, working from wrong side of garment.

Sleeve headings (pages 76 and 77) support gathered or pleated sleeve caps, such as those on pouf, leg-of-mutton, or juliet sleeves.

Special Techniques for Sleeves

Many sleeve styles are popular for special-occasion garments. On the following pages are construction techniques for several styles, including basic fitted sleeves, sleeves with button and loop closures, and sleeves with headings. Use these techniques to supplement or alter the pattern you are using.

In many cases, the technique you choose depends on the fabric you are using for the sleeves. If the fabric is sheer or fragile, you may add lining to the sleeves to eliminate the need for facings or hems. Lining also supports the fabric, especially important for fitted sleeves from lightweight lace, to prevent the lace from tearing when the garment is worn.

The point on the long, fitted sleeve of a bridal gown traditionally points to the ring finger. After trying on the muslin test garment, you may want to change the cutting line on the lower edge of the sleeve, to align the point, before cutting the actual garment fabric.

If you are adding lace openwork (page 106), complete the openwork before assembling the sleeve, for easier handling. To determine the placement of the lace motifs, pin the sleeve to the bodice or use the sleeve in the test garment. Take care to position the lace motifs so any sleeve facings or hems will not show through the lace openwork.

Basic fitted sleeves (pages 70 and 71) may be lined, using a hairline seam, a technique often used for sheer fabrics. Or they may be unlined and narrow-hemmed.

Sleeves with button and loop closures (pages 72 to 75) may be lined or faced, depending on the fabric used.

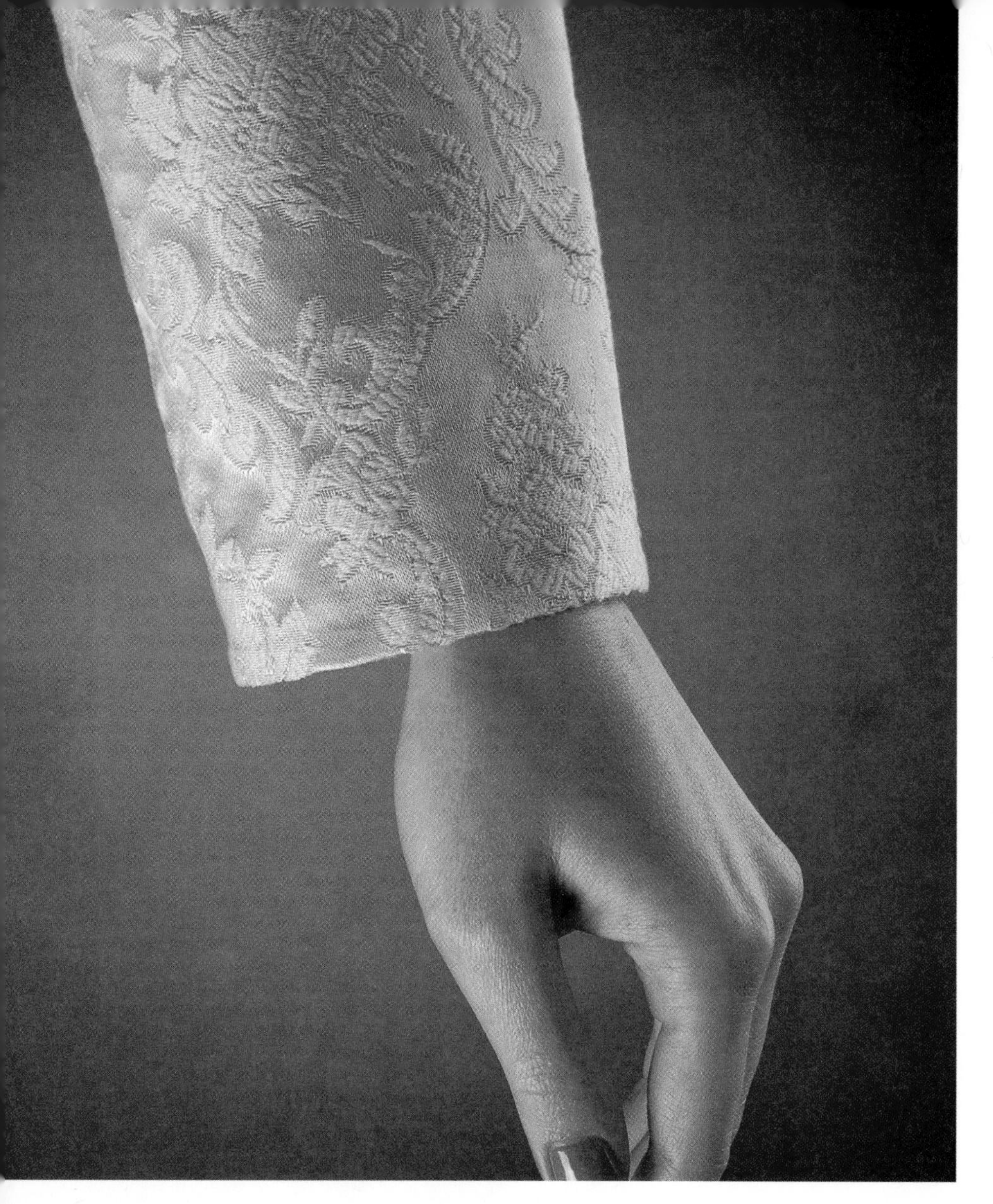

Sleeves with Narrow Hems

Narrow hand-stitched hems are often all that is necessary to finish the lower edge of tapered, unlined sleeves. For a smooth hem, it is important that the hem allowance be angled to fit the taper of the sleeve. Otherwise, the fabric will ripple between the stitches on the right side of the sleeve. If the pattern is not angled correctly, reshape the seam as shown in step 1, below.

The lower edge of the sleeve is folded under twice, using a 5⁄8" (1.5 cm) hem allowance, and the hem is hand-stitched in place. Suitable for most lightweight and mediumweight fabrics, the narrow double-fold hem results in a neat, finished look.

How to Sew a Sleeve with a Narrow Hem

1) Adjust sleeve length, if necessary. Trim pattern 5⁄8" (1.5 cm) beyond hemline; fold at hemline. Trace angle of seamline at side of hem allowance; cut on marked line.

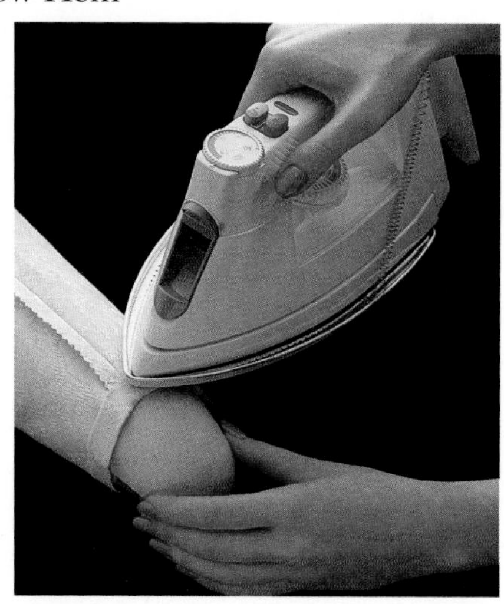

2) Cut out sleeve, using the adjusted pattern; stitch and press the sleeve seam. Press under 5⁄8" (1.5 cm) hem allowance on lower edge.

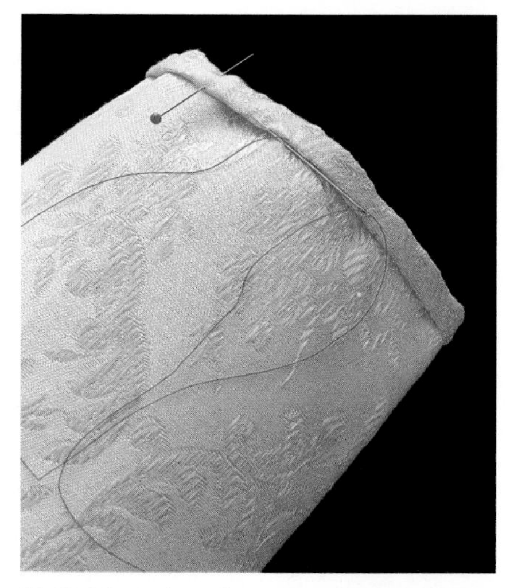

3) Fold under the raw edge to the pressed edge; pin in place. Slipstitch hem; press.

Lined Sheer Sleeves

Long, tapered sleeves and short cap sleeves in lightweight lace or sheer fabrics are quickly constructed when lined and finished with an inconspicuous hairline seam. The outer sleeve and the lining are stitched separately at the underarm seam, then joined with a hairline seam at the lower edge.

Select a soft net or organza for the lining of lace sleeves. To highlight the lace, organza in a contrasting color may be used. Sheer sleeves may be lined with self-fabric, net, or organza, depending on the desired effect. Cut the sleeve and the lining with a 5/8" (1.5 cm) seam allowance at the lower edge.

How to Sew a Lined Sheer Sleeve

1) Stitch underarm seam of sleeve, using double-stitched or French seam (pages 54 and 55). Repeat for sleeve lining.

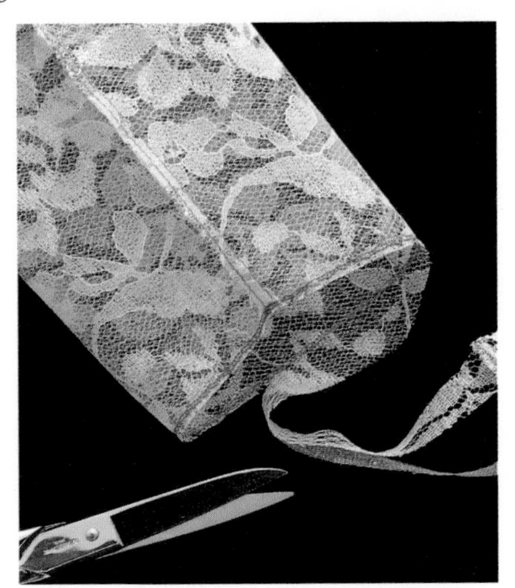

2) Pin the sleeve to lining at lower edge, right sides together. Stitch a hairline seam, using 5/8" (1.5 cm) seam allowance, and trim (page 55).

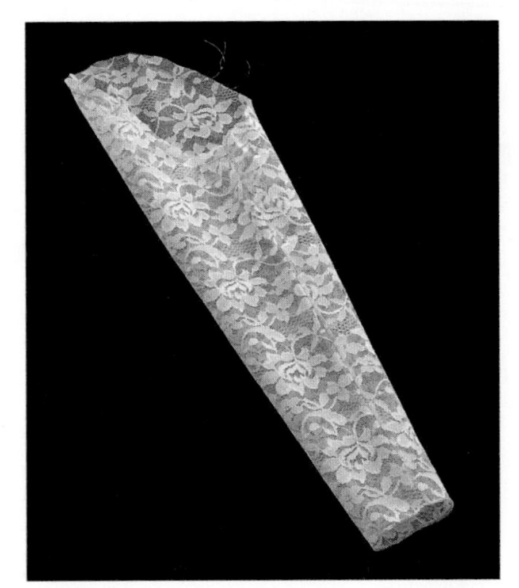

3) Turn sleeve right side out; press. Baste sleeve and lining together at the sleeve cap.

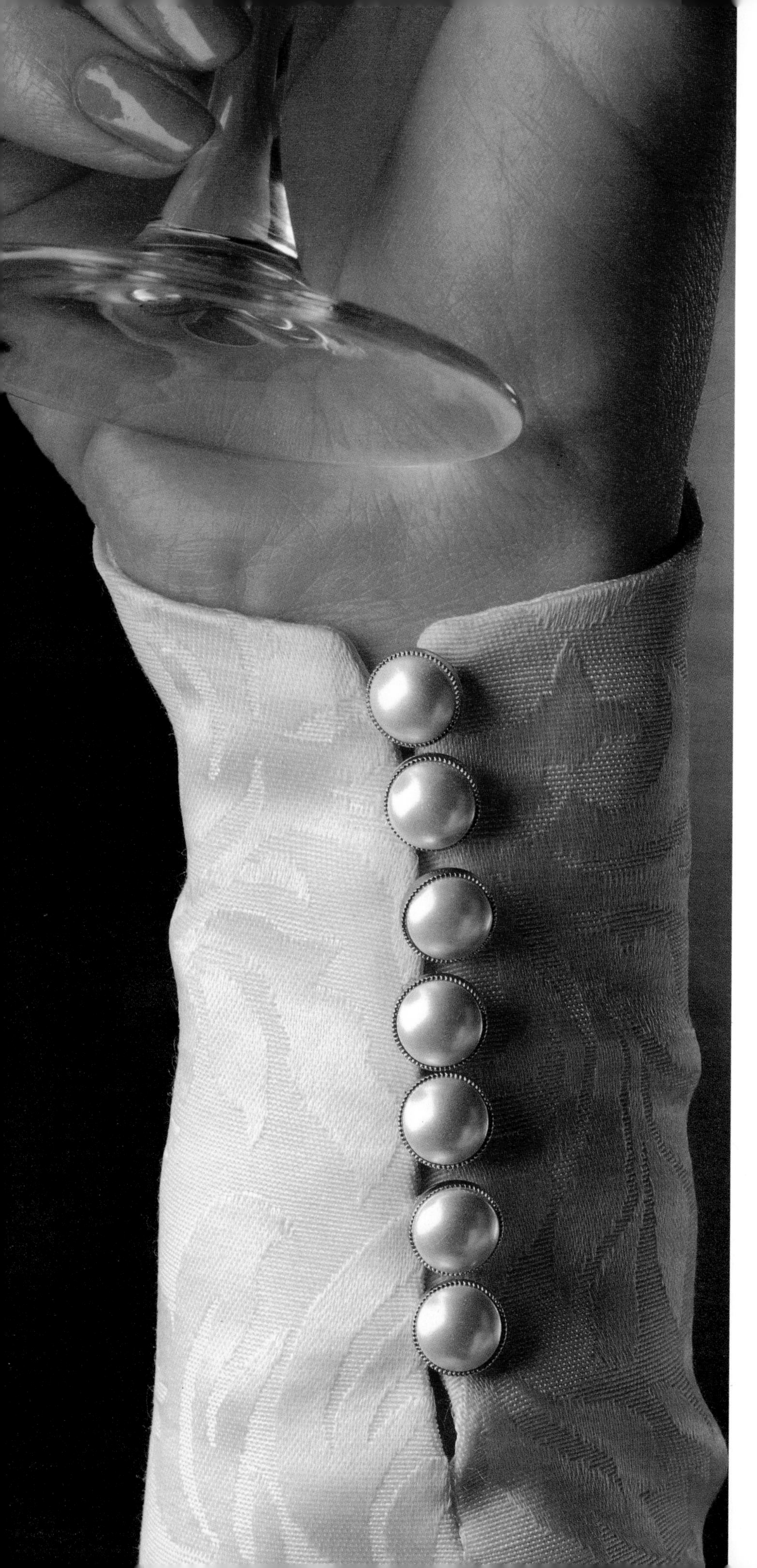

Sleeves with Button & Loop Closures

Small buttons with button loops are traditional wrist closures on sleeves of bridal gowns. For quick construction, use purchased button looping. This trim is available in several weights and with the loops spaced at various intervals. To reduce bulk, purchase lightweight button looping.

The technique for constructing sleeves with button and loop closures varies with the type of fabric. Sleeves from an opaque fabric, such as taffeta, satin, or brocade, are finished with a facing; if the pattern does not include a facing, you can easily make one, following the instructions opposite.

Lightweight lace and sheer sleeves are constructed with a lining of soft net or organza. The lining allows for easy construction at the wrist opening and stabilizes the lace. Sleeves from heavier lace, such as alencon, are constructed with an inconspicuous overlapped sleeve seam.

Any of these techniques may be used for the lower sleeve portion of a juliet sleeve (page 15). Construct the upper sleeve and attach it to the lower sleeve, following the pattern instructions.

How to Sew a Faced Sleeve with a Button and Loop Closure

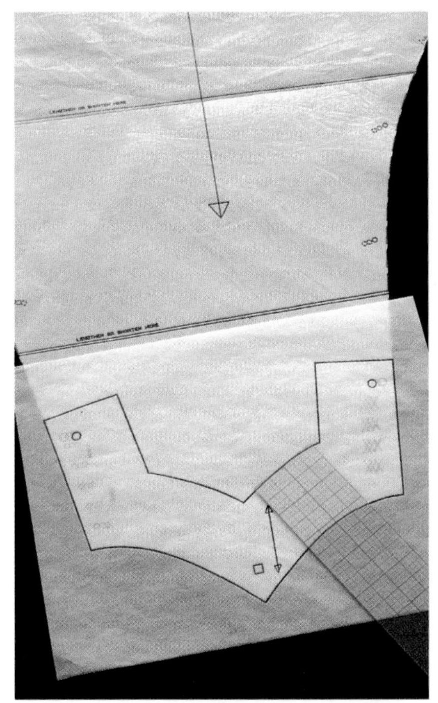

1) Make sleeve facing, if necessary, by tracing around bottom of sleeve pattern to 5/8" (1.5 cm) above the marking for wrist opening. Mark a line 2 1/8" (5.3 cm) inside the traced line; connect the ends of the lines.

2) Cut sleeve and facing; transfer markings for wrist opening. Finish the upper edges of facing.

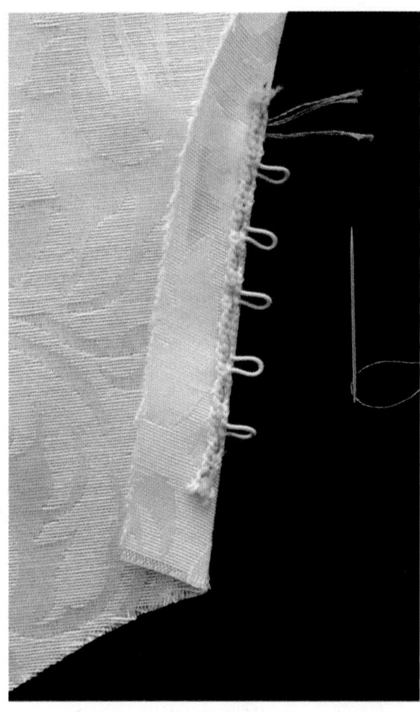

3) Press under 5/8" (1.5 cm) on back edge of sleeve along wrist opening. Pin button looping along pressed seamline, with loops extending beyond folded edge and first loop about 1" (2.5 cm) above raw edge; hand-baste to seam allowance.

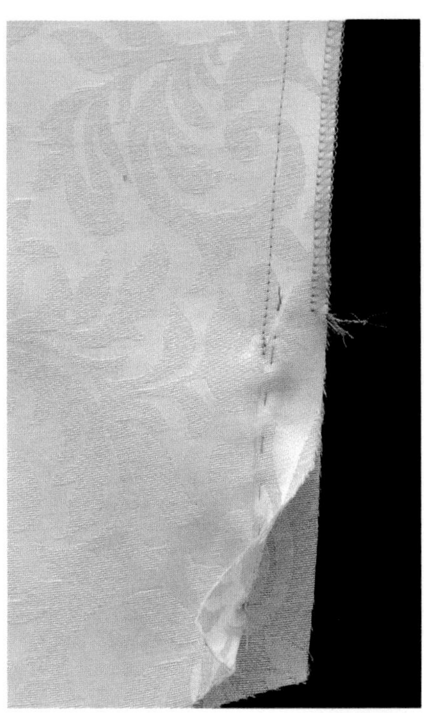

4) Stitch 5/8" (1.5 cm) seam above wrist opening. On fabrics that ravel easily, finish raw edges.

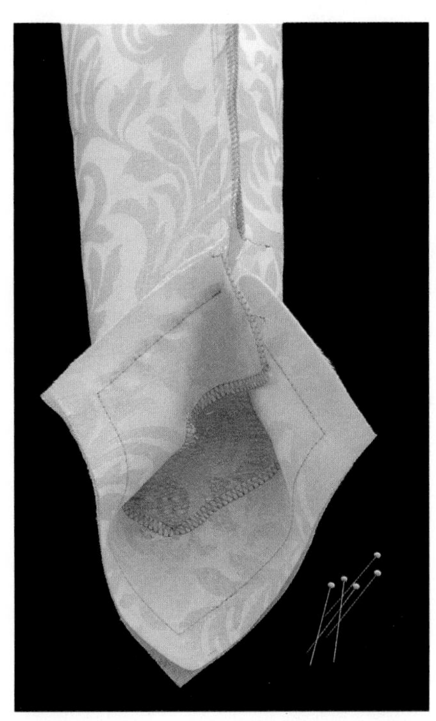

5) Pin the facing to the lower edge of sleeve, with right sides together and raw edges even. Stitch along wrist opening and lower edge.

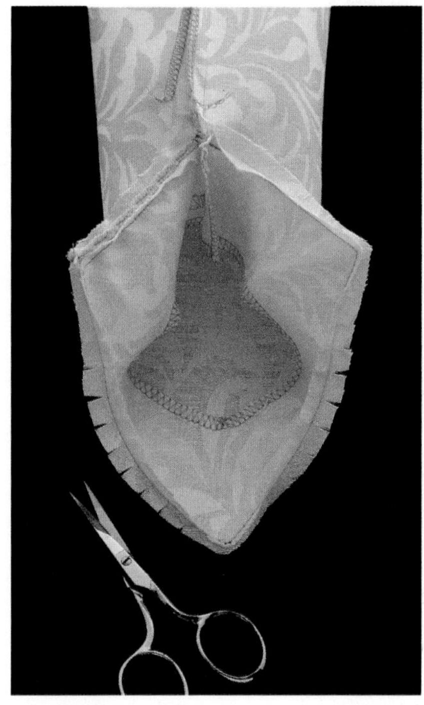

6) Press the seam allowances open. Trim seam allowances; trim corners and clip curves.

(Continued on next page)

How to Sew a Faced Sleeve with a Button and Loop Closure (continued)

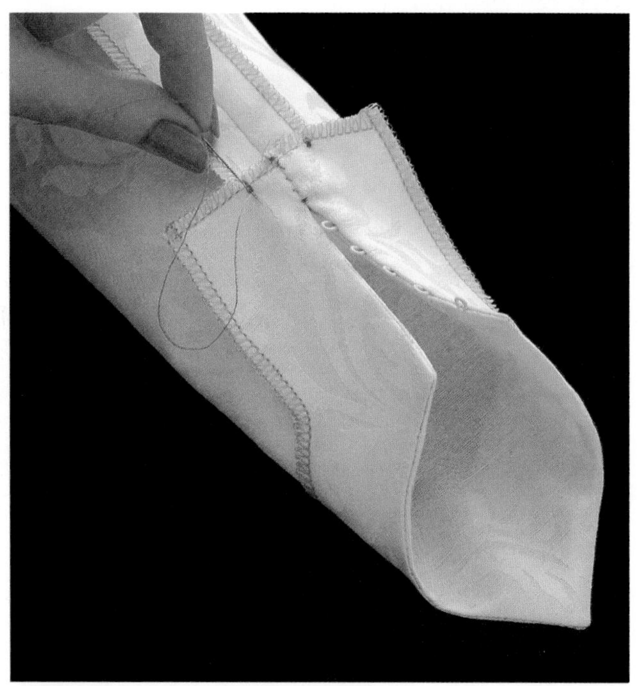

7) Turn and press facing, taking care not to imprint edges on right side of sleeve; press sleeve seam open. Tack facing to seam allowance, turning under ends and stitching them in place.

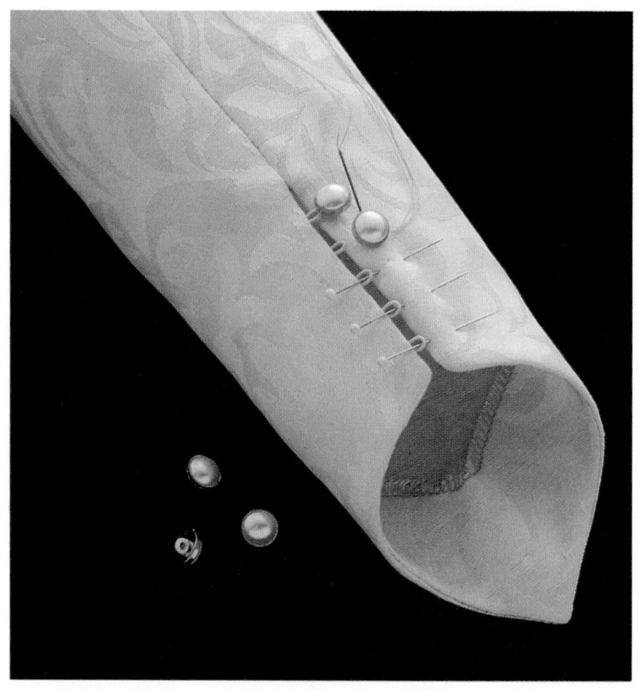

8) Turn sleeve right side out. Position wrist opening closed, and insert a pin through each button loop. Secure a button at each pin; continue stitching from button to button, sliding the needle between the sleeve and facing.

How to Sew a Lined Lightweight Lace or Sheer Sleeve with a Button and Loop Closure

1) Cut sleeves from lightweight lace or sheer outer fabric; cut sleeve linings. Clip-mark the lace at wrist opening. Staystitch along seamline for 1" (2.5 cm) to reinforce lace at clip marks. Apply button looping and stitch hairline seam as in steps 3 and 4, opposite.

2) Stitch sleeve seam, stitching the lace and lining as one layer. Secure buttons as in step 8, above. Hand-stitch lace appliqués (page 104) or lace edging (page 66) to lower edge, if desired.

How to Sew a Lined Alençon Lace Sleeve with a Button and Loop Closure

1) Cut lace sleeve, using pattern; cut the back sleeve seam above the wrist opening following design of lace. Clip-mark lace sleeve at wrist opening. Cut sleeve lining from net or organza, using lace sleeves as the pattern.

2) Thread-trace sleeve seamlines above wrist opening on lace sleeve. Staystitch along seamlines for 1" (2.5 cm) to reinforce the lace at the clip marks. (Contrasting threads were used to show detail.)

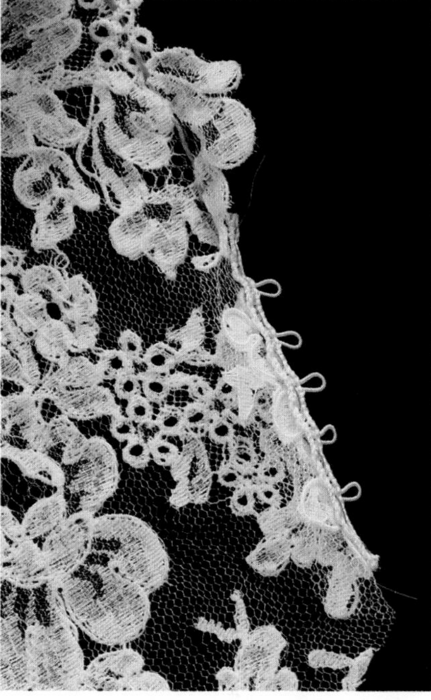

3) Press under 5/8" (1.5 cm) on the back edge of sleeve along the wrist opening. Pin button looping to the seam allowance, with loops extending beyond pressed edge and first loop about 1" (2 .5 cm) above raw edge. Hand-baste trim to seam allowance.

4) Pin lining to lace sleeve, with right sides together and raw edges even. Stitch hairline seam (page 55) along wrist opening and lower edge. Turn sleeve right side out; press. Baste sleeve and lining together.

5) Lap the back of sleeve over front, aligning thread-traced seamlines and easing fullness at elbow; baste. Using a backstitch, hand-stitch near outer edge of lace motifs on top of sleeve.

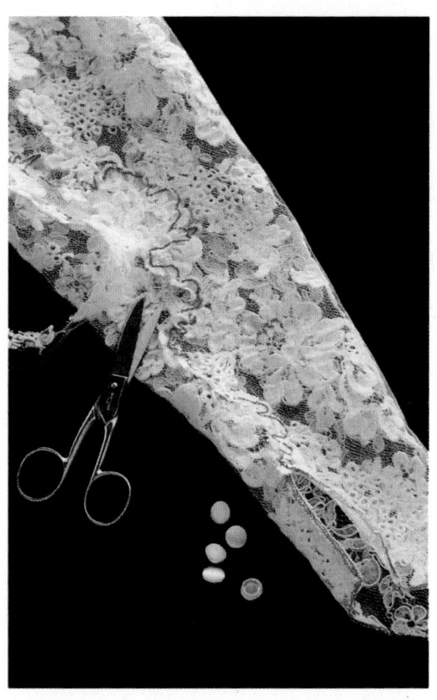

6) Remove basting; trim sleeve seam along lace motifs, next to stitching. Secure the buttons as in step 8, opposite. Hand-stitch lace appliqués (page 104) or lace edging (page 66) to lower edge, if desired.

Sleeve Headings

Sleeve headings extend into the sleeve to lift and support the sleeve cap. Sleeve headings are usually included in patterns; however, depending on the sleeve style and garment fabric used, they may not be full enough or extend far enough into the sleeve to provide the necessary support. You may want to make your own sleeve heading pattern.

Make the sleeve heading from a fabric or interfacing appropriate for the garment fabric. Sheer and lace sleeves require headings made from sheer fabric, such as cancan net, nylon organdy, or polyester organza, so the heading is not distracting. Cancan net provides the firmest support; cover the heading with polyester organza to prevent the net from irritating the skin. Nylon organdy also provides firm support for sheer sleeves. For light support on close-fitting sleeves, use a polyester organza. Nonwoven interfacings work well for sleeve headings in opaque fabrics, such as satins, taffetas, brocades, and velvets; use a heavyweight interfacing for the firmest support.

Check the length and width of the heading included in the pattern. Headings for large pouf sleeves usually extend 3" to 4" (7.5 to 10 cm) into the sleeve and are about twice the length of the distance between the gathering markings. Pin the heading in place, and check the sleeve support; you may want to try a heading in a different size or fabric.

How to Make a Pattern for a Sleeve Heading

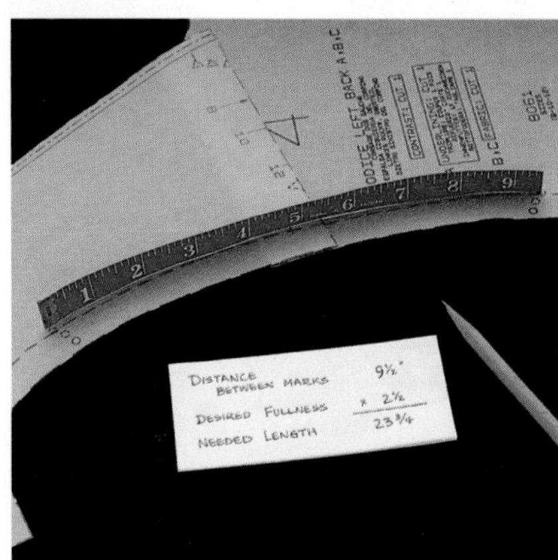

1) Measure the distance between gathering markings on armhole seamline; multiply this measurement times 2 or 2½, to determine the length of the heading.

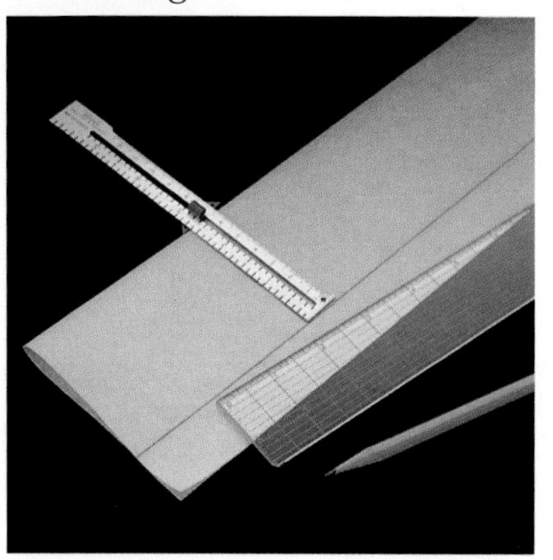

2) Cut a sheet of paper to length of heading; fold in half lengthwise. Mark a line, parallel to the fold, at desired depth of sleeve heading plus ⅝" (1.5 cm) for seam allowance.

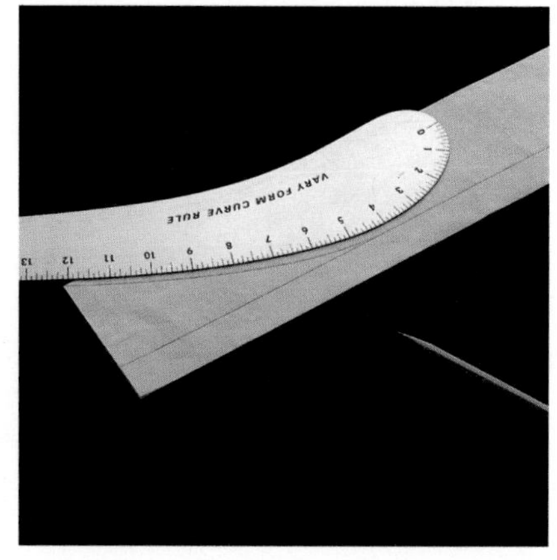

3) Mark curved lines to the fold as shown, to taper ends. Cut along marked lines through both layers.

How to Sew a Sleeve Heading

1) Cut sleeve heading, using pattern; woven fabrics are generally cut on the bias. For cancan net heading, cut another piece from polyester organza; pin layers together.

2) Fold heading in half lengthwise, *wrong* sides together. Stitch two rows of gathering threads, ⅜" and ⅝" (1 and 1.5 cm) from raw edges.

3) Mark the center of the stitched edge with a pin; gather the heading to a length of about 6" (15 cm).

4) Position sleeve inside garment, exposing armhole seam allowance. Pin heading to seam allowance at top of sleeve, matching raw edges; place center of heading at shoulder seam.

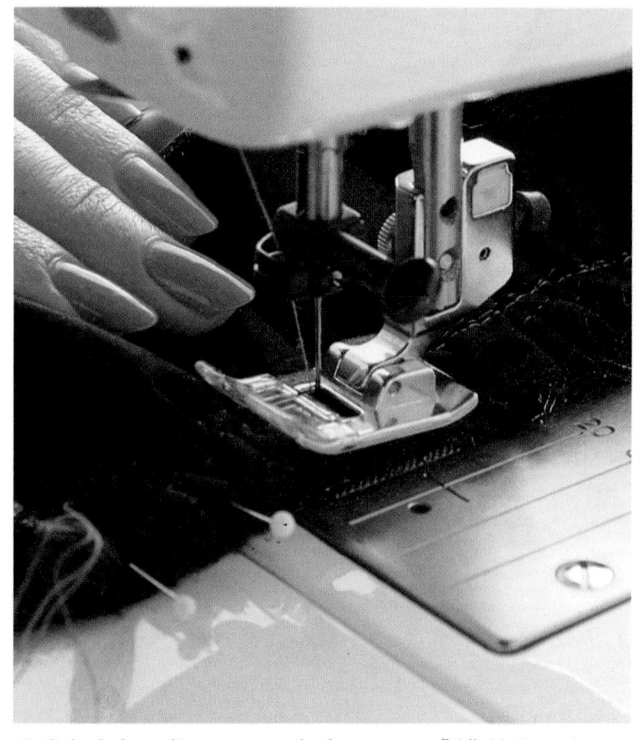

5) Stitch heading to armhole a scant ⅝" (1.5 cm) from raw edges. Trim seam allowances of heading and armhole to ¼" (6 mm). Bind seam allowances (page 57), if desired, using tricot bias binding.

Special Techniques for Closures

A closure on a special-occasion garment may be as inconspicuous as an invisible zipper, or may be as decorative as a button and loop closure. Choose a closure that complements the style of the gown and is suitable for the fabric.

The closures on the following pages use new, streamlined construction techniques that minimize the risk of marring specialty fabrics. Become familiar with the techniques you plan to use before you cut the fabric or plan the order of construction, because some closures require cutting or assembly changes.

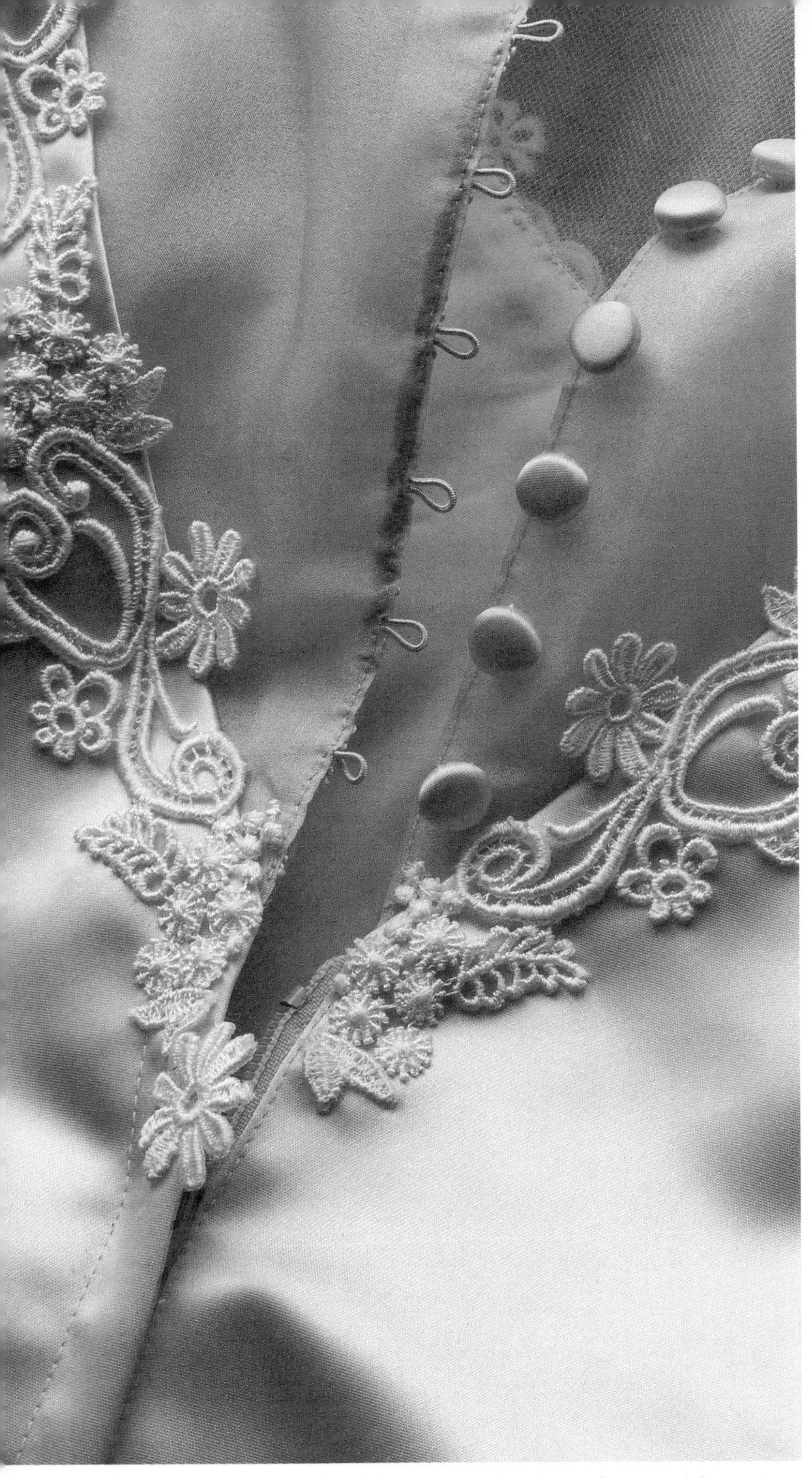

Lapped zipper (pages 80 and 81) is a popular closure for a special-occasion garment. Buttons and loops are used for the closure on the illusion neckline (page 89).

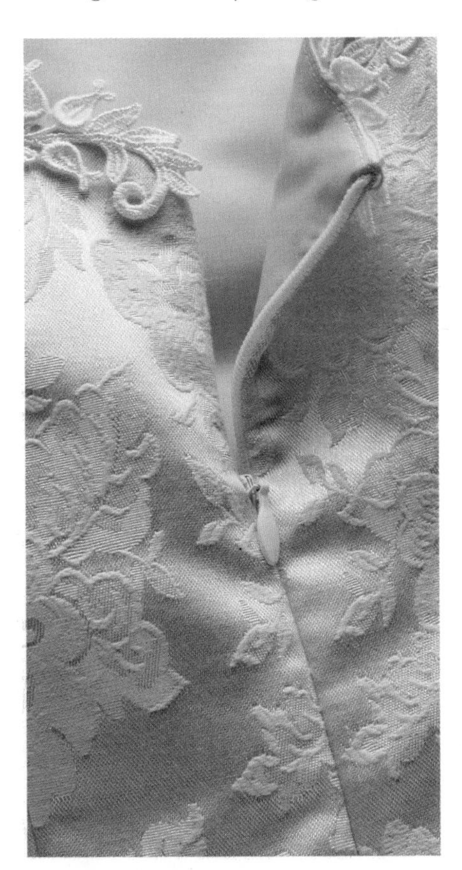

Invisible zipper (pages 82 and 83) provides an inconspicuous closure on fabrics with surface interest, such as brocades, sequined fabrics, and velvets.

Buttons, loops, and zipper (pages 85 to 87) are combined for a decorative closure with no visible stitching.

Lapped Zipper Closures

For special-occasion fabrics that tend to needle-mark and crease, the usual method for inserting a zipper is not recommended. In the method shown here, the seam allowances are pressed, allowing for the overlap; then the zipper is positioned and stitched in place. You may want to allow 1" (2.5 cm) seam allowances at the center back; this ensures that the seam allowance will be caught in the stitching if the fabric ravels.

When you are applying a lapped zipper to a garment with a deep V neckline, stitch the neckline seam up to the center back seamline and leave the seam allowances unstitched. This makes it easier to finish the inside of the garment.

Insert the zipper, keeping the lining fabric folded out of the way. If the zipper extends into the skirt, leave a longer opening in the skirt lining, making it easier to keep the lining free. Place the zipper stop ⅜" (1 cm) below the finished upper edge, to allow space for a hook and eye. If a zipper is inserted into a skirt with an overlay, it is stitched to the underskirt only, leaving the overlay free.

Lapped zipper is a popular closure. For a mock button and loop closure, stitch buttons on the lapped side.

How to Insert a Lapped Zipper

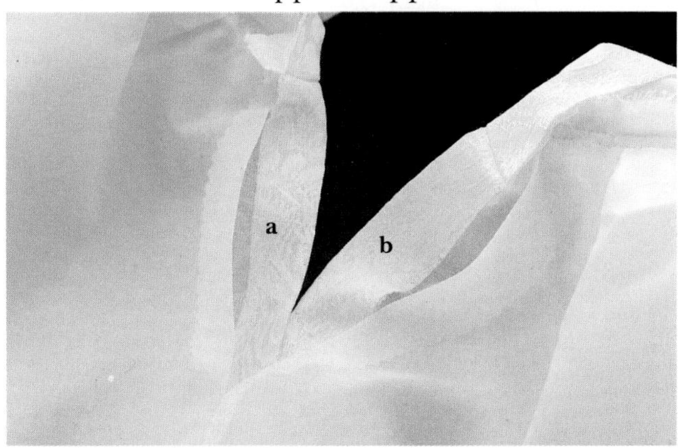

1) Mark position for bottom stop on seam allowance. Stitch seam up to mark. Press right seam allowance **(a)** 1/8" (3 mm) inside seamline; if 1" (2.5 cm) seam allowances are used, press under 7/8" (2.2 cm). Press left seam allowance **(b)** under along seamline.

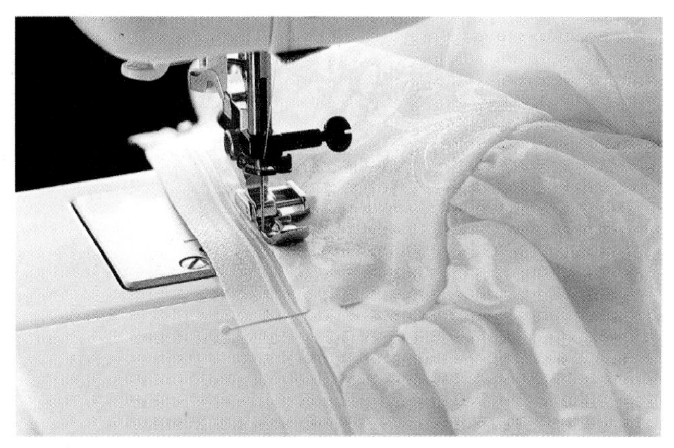

2) Place closed zipper, face up, under the folded edge on right back, with top zipper stop 3/8" (1 cm) from finished upper edge and fold close to zipper teeth; pin or baste in place. Check to make sure that zipper opens smoothly. Edgestitch, starting at the upper edge, using zipper foot.

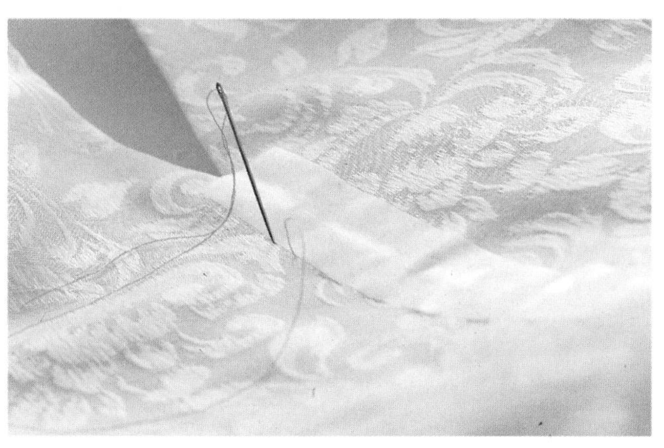

3) Lap folded edge on left back over folded edge on right back, concealing stitches; secure with transparent tape or pins. Hand-baste the left side of the zipper tape in place.

4) Open zipper. Stitch zipper in place, stitching a scant 1/2" (1.3 cm) from folded edge. When stitching is near zipper tab, stop stitching, with needle down in fabric. Lift presser foot, and slide zipper tab above needle.

5) Continue stitching, pivoting at bottom of zipper opening.

6) Stitch the lining in place as on page 87, step 10. Attach hook and eye on wrong side of garment at the neckline.

Skirt with overlay. Follow steps 1 to 4, stitching from upper edge to the waistline seam; secure thread. Fold skirt overlay over bodice; finish as in steps 5 and 6.

Invisible Zippers

Invisible zippers provide a garment closure that is inconspicuous. Once the zipper is inserted, the pull tab is the only visible feature. Invisible zippers are an excellent alternative to traditional zippers on fabrics with surface interest, such as brocades, velvets, and sequined fabrics.

Invisible zippers are available in several lengths and colors. If you cannot find a color to match the fabric, paint the pull tab, using an enamel paint.

A special presser foot is required for inserting an invisible zipper. This foot unrolls the coil; after stitching, the coil and fabric roll to the inside, concealing the zipper. The presser foot is easily assembled to fit the shank length and needle slant of the sewing machine.

Invisible zippers can be most easily inserted by stitching them into the garment before stitching any part of the seam.

How to Insert an Invisible Zipper

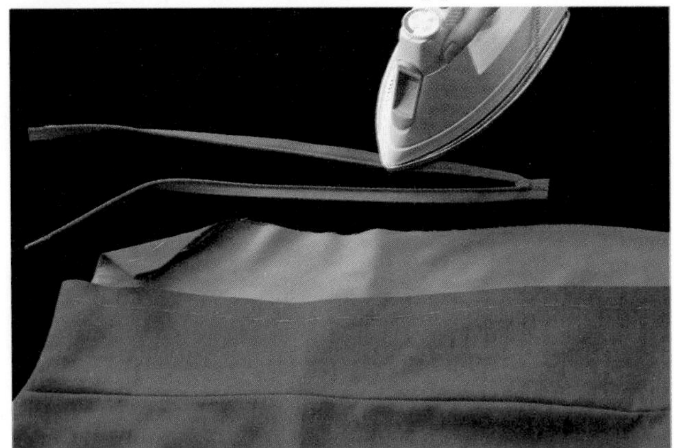

1) Hand-baste a line the length of the zipper on garment pieces, a scant ¾" (2 cm) from the raw edge. Open zipper. Steam press zipper tape from wrong side, to unroll coils.

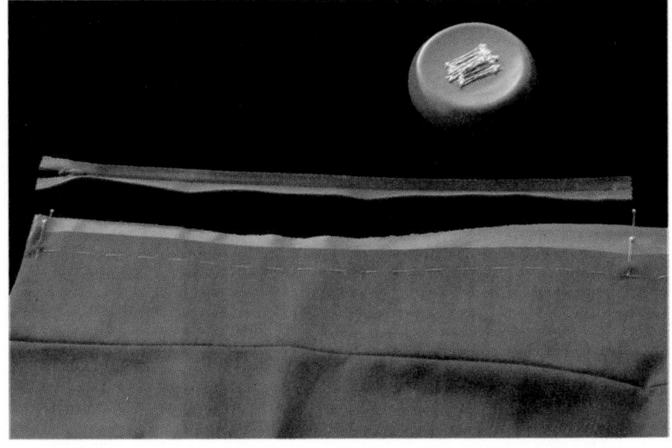

2) Position closed zipper on the right side of the garment section, with zipper tab ⅜" (1 cm) from neckline seam; pin-mark garment pieces at upper and lower edges of zipper, making sure the pattern markings are aligned.

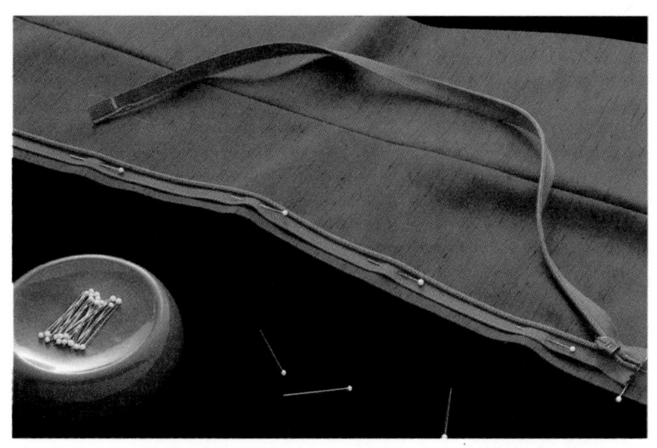

3) Open zipper; position on right garment section, right sides together, with left side of the zipper coil aligned to basted line and ends of zipper aligned to pin marks; zipper tape is in seam allowance. Pin or hand-baste zipper tape in place.

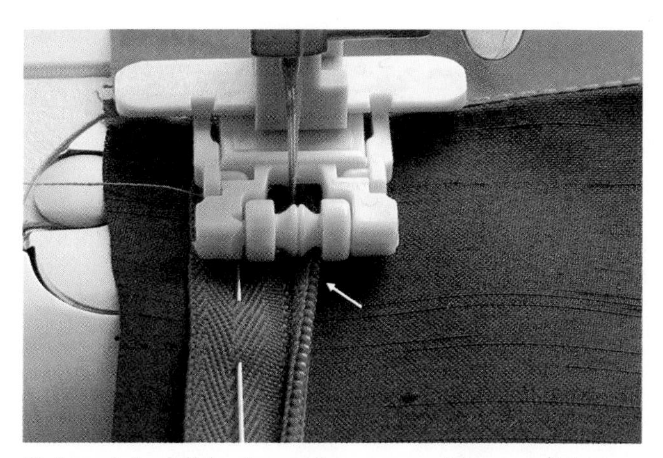

4) Attach invisible zipper foot to machine; position zipper coil under groove on right side of foot (arrow). Slide zipper foot on adapter to adjust needle position so stitching will be very close to the coil; on heavier fabric, set needle position slightly farther from coil.

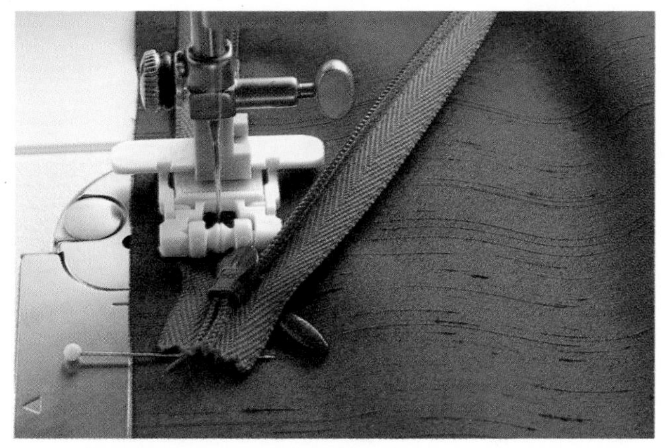

5) Stitch, starting at upper edge of zipper coil, until zipper foot touches the pull tab at bottom, taking care not to stretch fabric. Secure thread at ends.

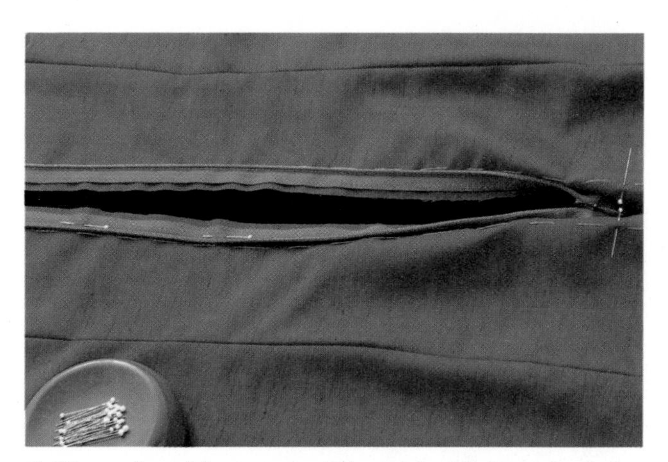

6) Pin or hand-baste remaining side of zipper to left garment section, as in step 3, making sure to align ends of zipper to pin marks.

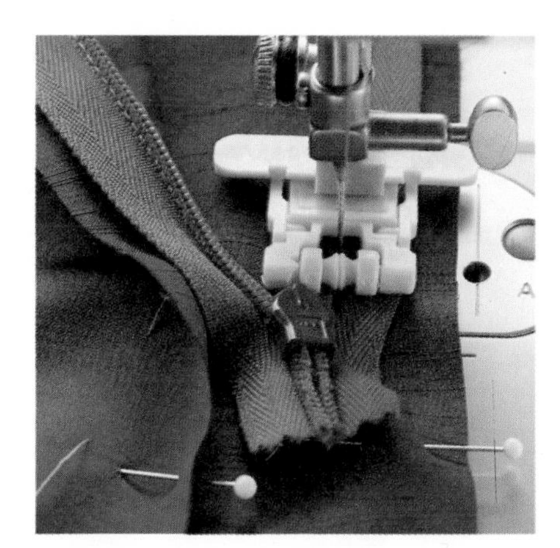

7) Position coil under zipper foot; slide zipper foot on adapter to the opposite side, and adjust the needle position. Stitch until zipper foot touches the pull tab; secure thread.

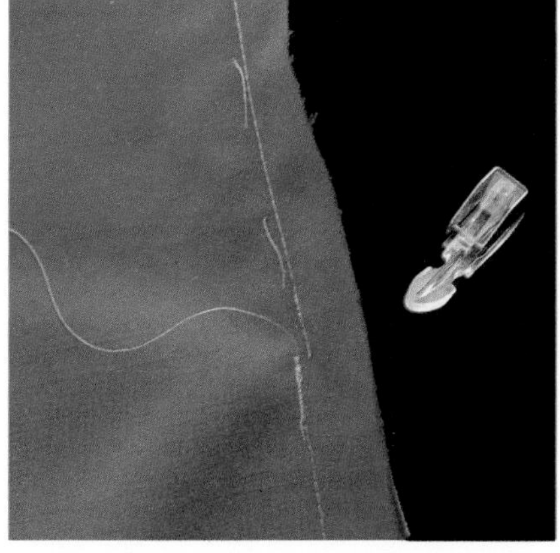

8) Close the zipper and stitch the remainder of garment seam; use a regular zipper foot to get as close as possible to the zipper seam.

9) Secure lower end of tape to seam allowances, using a regular zipper foot. Stitch the lining in place as on page 49, step 3. Attach hook and eye on inside of the garment at the neckline.

Zipper Closures with Buttons & Loops

Buttons and loops give special attention to the center back of a gown. Combining button looping with a hidden zipper, the technique that follows provides a secure closure with no visible stitching on the right side of the garment. The zipper makes it easier to fasten the buttons.

For this technique, it is necessary to add underlining to the bodice, and, if the closure extends into the skirt, a skirt lining is also necessary. This closure also requires wider seam allowances at the center back.

Use button looping with elastic loops that are spaced at ½" (1.3 cm) intervals. Before the neckline seam is stitched, the button looping is applied and covered with a tricot bias binding. The zipper is inserted like a fly-front zipper.

Zipper is hidden under buttons and loops, giving a strong back closure that is also decorative.

How to Insert a Zipper Closure with Buttons and Loops

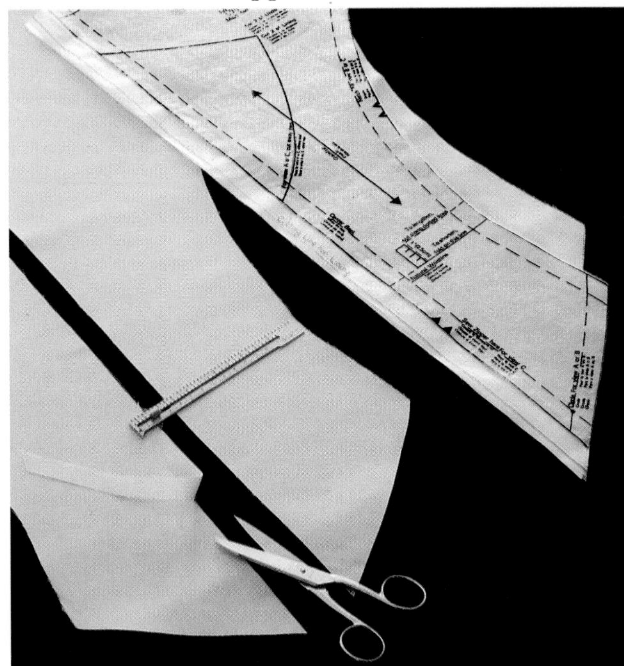

1) For closure in the bodice only. Cut the bodice and the underlining, allowing 1½" (3.8 cm) seam allowances at center back. Cut lining with 1¼" (3.2 cm) seam allowances at center back; trim ⅝" (1.5 cm) from seam allowance on left bodice back lining. Baste underlining to bodice pieces. Assemble bodice as on pages 43 and 44, steps 1 to 4.

2) Stitch center back seam below marking for closure. Press under 1½" (3.8 cm) seam allowance on left bodice back. Position button looping on the seam allowance, with the loops extending beyond pressed edge and first loop about 1" (2.5 cm) below the raw edge; hand-baste to seam allowance only.

(Continued on next page)

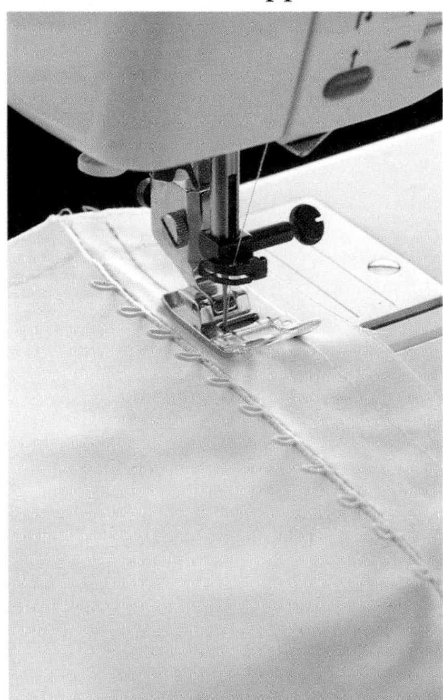

3) Position tricot bias binding on button looping. Machine-stitch along both edges of the binding, catching button looping in first row of stitching. Remove basting stitches from step 2.

4) Assemble collar, if included in pattern; insert button looping in the back seam. Assemble lining. Stitch neckline seam. Trim and clip seam; understitch (page 57). Set in sleeves.

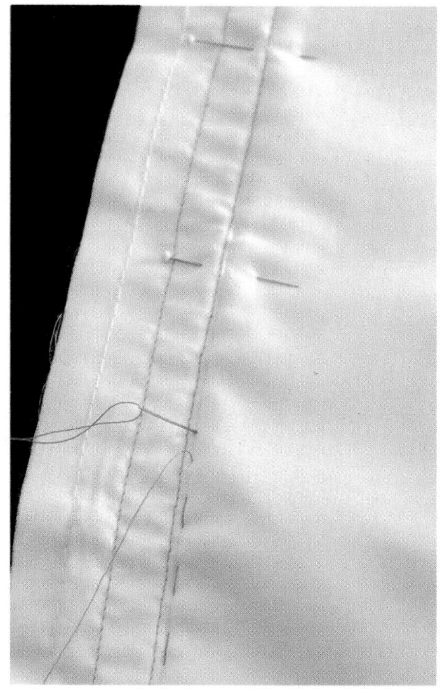

5) Hand-baste 1½" (3.8 cm) center back seam, or machine-baste it if fabric does not needle-mark. Lightly press seam open.

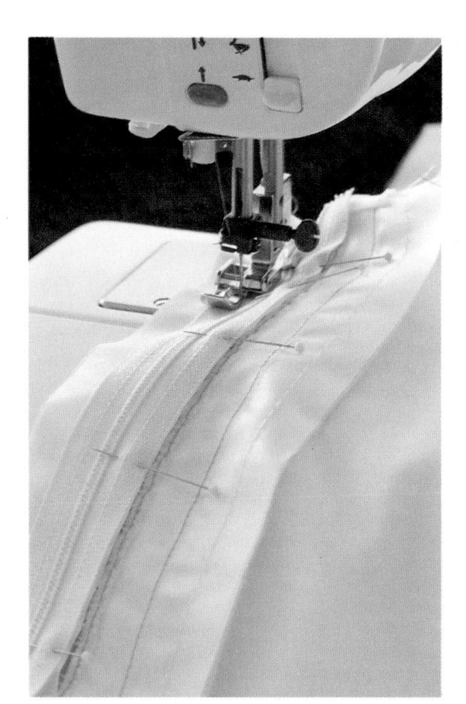

6) Place closed zipper face down on seam allowance, aligning right side of zipper tape to seamline; pin to the seam allowance. Using a zipper foot, stitch the left side of zipper tape to seam allowance.

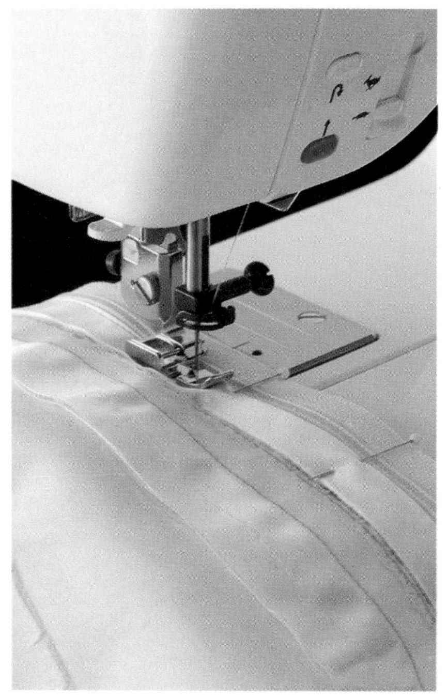

7) Turn the zipper right side up; edgestitch next to foldline, stitching through the zipper tape and seam allowance only.

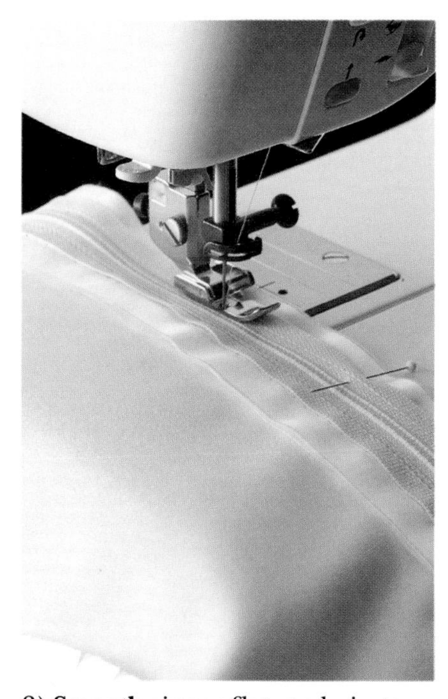

8) Smooth zipper flat, and pin to remaining seam allowance. Stitch close to the zipper teeth, stitching through the zipper tape and seam allowance only.

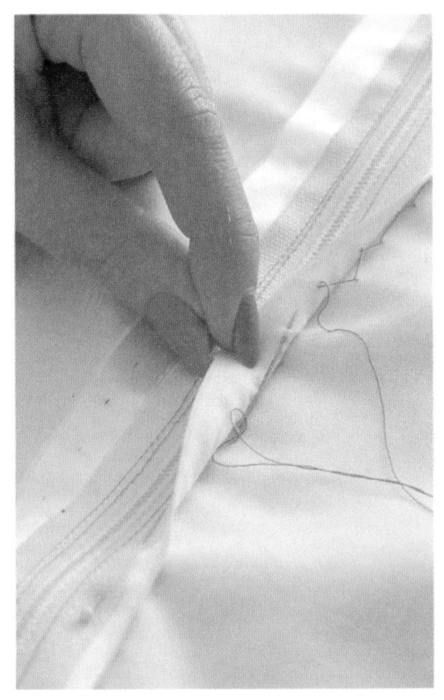

9) Stitch the seam allowance to the underlining along both sides of the zipper tape, using catchstitch (page 92). Remove basting.

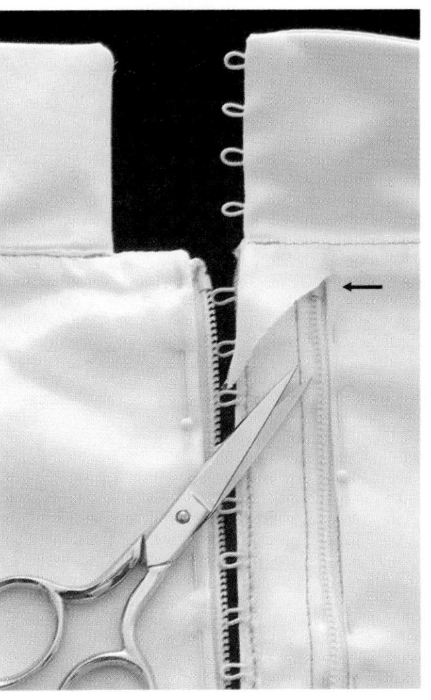

10) Fold under seam allowances of lining at center back; on the left bodice back, clip diagonally to the zipper stop (arrow). Trim excess at clip. Fold under; pin and stitch in place.

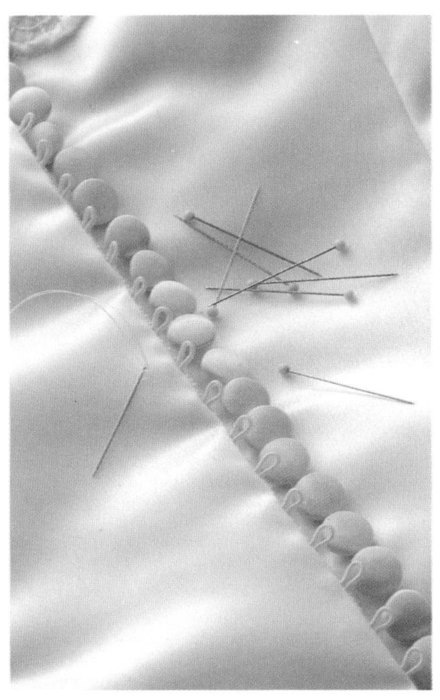

11) Mark position for satin-covered buttons with pins. Secure buttons at markings. Fasten buttons, using small crochet hook or tweezers.

For closure that extends into skirt.
1) Follow step 1 on page 85. Cut skirt and lining, allowing 1½" (3.8 cm) seam allowances at center back. Stitch for 2" (5 cm) at clip mark for closure on skirt; clip to stitching ½" (1.3 cm) below mark.

2) Follow steps 2 to 4 on pages 85 and 86. Fold skirt and lining fabrics together above clip in skirt. Assemble and attach skirt as on pages 46 and 47, steps 1 to 3; do not fold back seam allowance of lining in step 3.

3) Follow steps 5 to 11, opposite, catchstitching the zipper tape to the bodice underlining and skirt lining. At center back, trim seam allowances to ⅝" (1.5 cm) below the zipper.

Button & Loop Closures for Illusion Necklines

Button looping is traditionally used for the back closure of an illusion neckline. Assemble the bodice as on page 45, using sheer fabric or illusion net for the outer fabric of the upper bodice, and soft net or organza for the lining. To prevent strain on the fabric, the edges of the opening are reinforced with horsehair braid. A lapped zipper (pages 80 and 81) is usually inserted in the lower bodice and skirt.

How to Sew a Button and Loop Closure for an Illusion Neckline

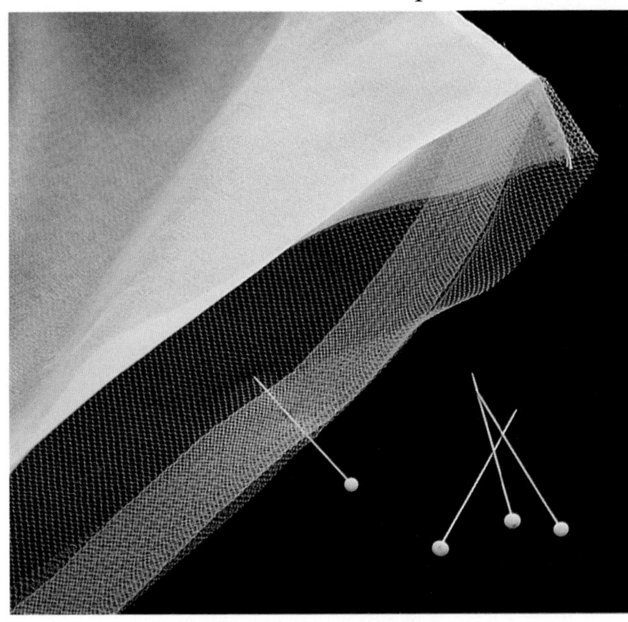

1) Cut ½" (1.3 cm) horsehair braid to the length of illusion neckline opening. Position horsehair braid inside lining seam allowance of left bodice back; pin or baste in place. (For this garment, sheer fabric is used for the outer fabric and net for the lining.)

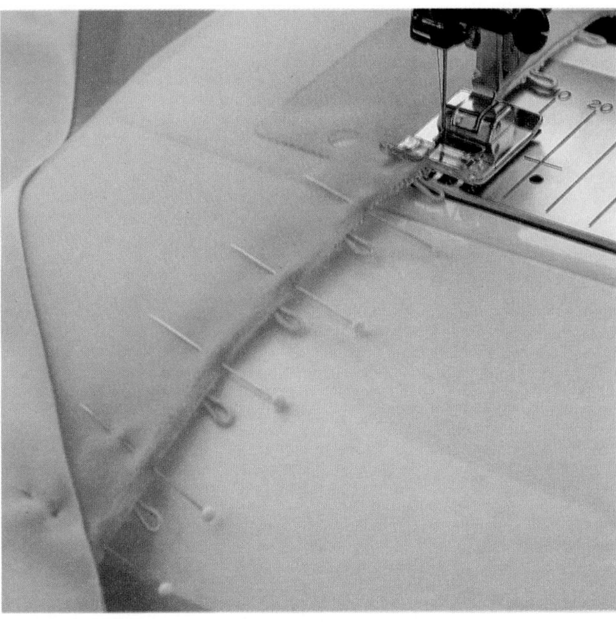

2) Cut button looping, and insert between the outer fabric and lining at left bodice opening, with loops extending beyond pressed edges; position first loop about ⅜" (1 cm) below finished upper edge. Pin or baste trim in place. Edgestitch.

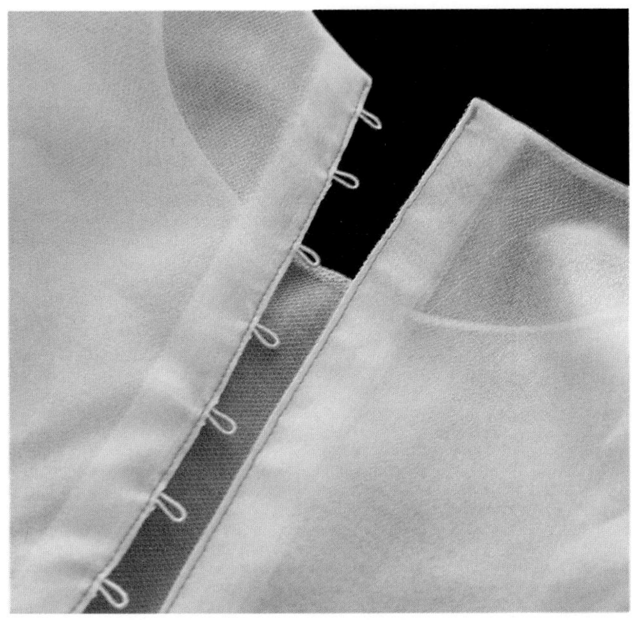

3) Cut horsehair braid, and position it inside lining seam allowance of right bodice back; pin or baste in place. Edgestitch.

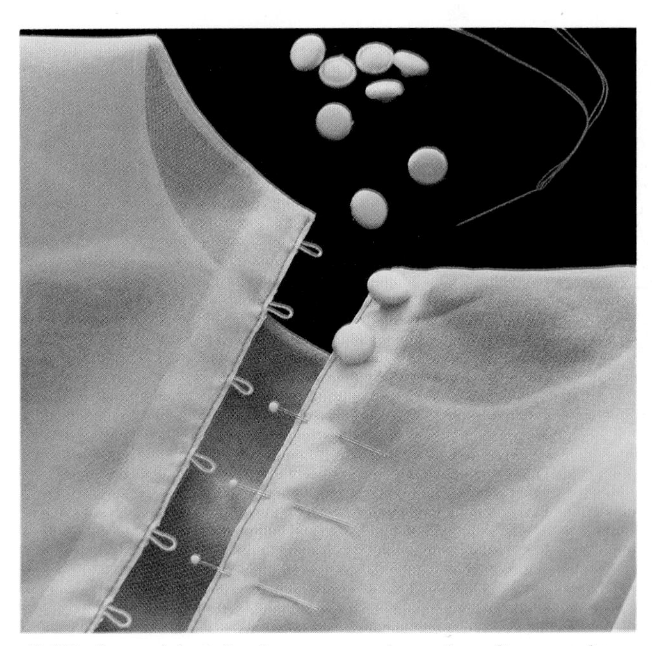

4) Mark position for buttons, using pins. Secure the buttons at the pin marks. Fasten the buttons, using a small crochet hook or tweezers.

Skirt Hems

On special-occasion garments, stitch hems so they are as inconspicuous as possible. Select the hem method that is appropriate for the fabric and the garment. In general, the more flared the skirt, the narrower the hem.

Types of Hems

Narrow machine-stitched hem is nonbulky and is used for sheer and silky fabrics. It is also suitable for satin, taffeta, and organza. It is an easy hem finish for flared skirts.

Horsehair braid hem gives body and fullness to skirts. It helps to prevent long skirts from channeling between the legs and to keep trains flared. Select the width of the horsehair braid according to the weight of the fabric and the amount of body desired. For lightweight fabrics, use ½" or 1" (1.3 or 2.5 cm) horsehair braid. For more support on mediumweight to heavyweight fabrics, use 2" or 3" (5 or 7.5 cm) horsehair braid.

Catchstitched hem has crisscrossing stitches that are worked between the hem edge and the garment; this prevents the hem edge from making a ridge on the right side and has built-in give to reduce strain on the fabric. Catchstitched hems are used for velvets and other fabrics that tend to overpress easily. They are also helpful for hemming slim skirts, which tend to be subjected to stress.

Faced hem is used for hemming sequined fabrics. With this technique, a facing is substituted for the self-fabric hem allowances, to reduce bulk and to prevent sequins from irritating the skin. For the facing, use a purchased hem tape or 2" (5 cm) bias strips cut from lightweight fabric. Facings are used to hem skirts and sleeves as well as the lower edges of blouses and jackets from sequined fabrics.

Double-fold hem is appropriate for straight hem edges in sheer and lightweight fabrics. The raw edge of the fabric is enclosed and does not show through to the right side of the garment. The double fold also adds weight to the hem edge. Do not use this hem in A-line or princess styles, because hems in these styles should drape softly.

Rolled overlock hem is a quick and easy narrow hem for lightweight fabrics. Sewn on an overlock machine, or serger, it is an appropriate finish for the edges of ruffles, slips, and skirt linings.

Topstitched hem is appropriate for linings on special-occasion garments. Finish the raw edge of the fabric with an overlock stitch, or fold under the raw edge ¼" (6 mm).

Tips for Sewing Hems

Allow the garment to hang for at least 24 hours before marking the hem, especially if it has a bias or circular skirt.

Mark the hem while wearing the undergarments, petticoat, and shoes you plan to wear. Stand on a hard floor; if you stand on carpet, the markings may be inaccurate.

Hem floor-length gowns ½" to ¾" (1.3 to 2 cm) from the floor. Hem tea-length gowns about 8" to 11" (20.5 to 28 cm) from the floor, choosing the length that is most flattering for you.

Hem skirt linings ⅜" to ½" (1 to 1.3 cm) shorter than the skirt.

Use a lightweight thread for inconspicuous hand stitches. Catch only one or two threads of the fabric in each stitch; avoid pulling the thread too tight.

Press hems carefully to prevent a ridge along the edge of the hem. If more than one person is sewing bridesmaids' dresses, make sure the same hemming technique is used for all the gowns.

Bridal gowns are hemmed so the skirt length tapers gradually into the train. Hold your arms in a natural position at your sides, while the hem is marked to floor length in the front skirt area between your arms.

How to Sew a Narrow Machine-stitched Hem

1) Mark hem 1/8" (3 mm) longer than the finished hem length; press in place. Stitch close to fold, using short stitch length. Trim excess fabric close to stitching, using appliqué scissors. Press to remove fullness, if fabric has stretched.

2) Turn hem edge to wrong side, enclosing raw edge. Stitch an even distance from folded edge.

How to Sew a Horsehair Braid Hem

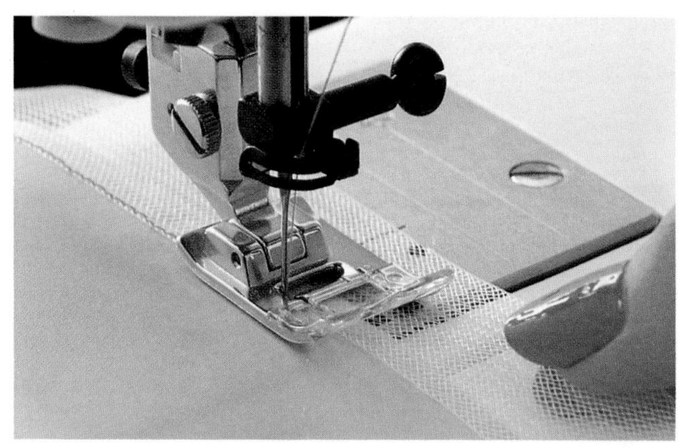

1) Trim fabric 1/4" (6 mm) below the finished hem length. Place horsehair braid on right side of fabric, overlapping fabric 1/4" (6 mm); stitch close to edge, stretching horsehair braid slightly.

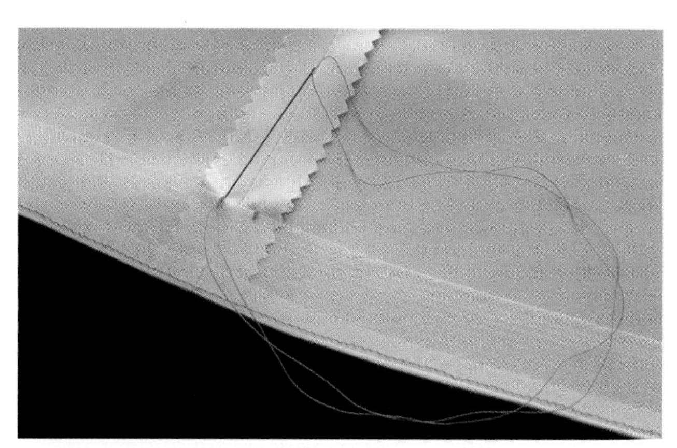

2) Press horsehair braid to wrong side; slipstitch hem, or hand-tack braid to seam allowances only. Floor-length gowns should be slipstitched to avoid catching the hem with shoes.

How to Sew a Catchstitched Hem

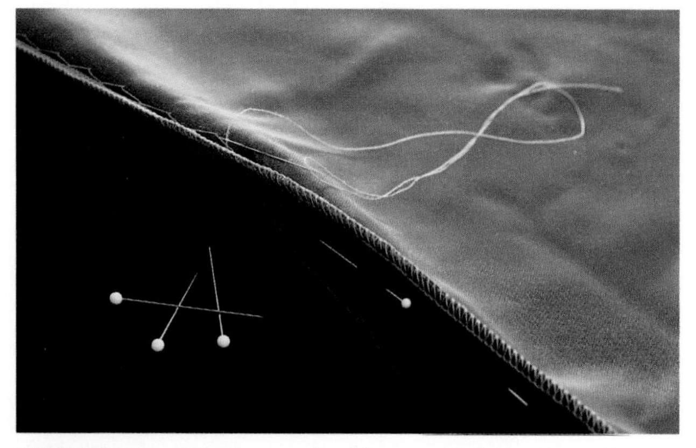

1) Finish raw edge by overlocking or pinking. Press hem in place. Fold back hem edge. Working from left to right, catch the fabric alternately at hem edge and garment, taking small backstitches; do not pull stitches tight.

2) Press the hem from wrong side of garment; place velvet on needleboard or scrap of self-fabric. To set hemline in velvet, pat along the foldline with a stiff-bristled brush.

How to Sew a Faced Hem

1) Trim fabric ¼" (6 mm) below the finished hem length; remove sequins as necessary. Stitch bias hem facing to garment, using ¼" (6 mm) seam allowance.

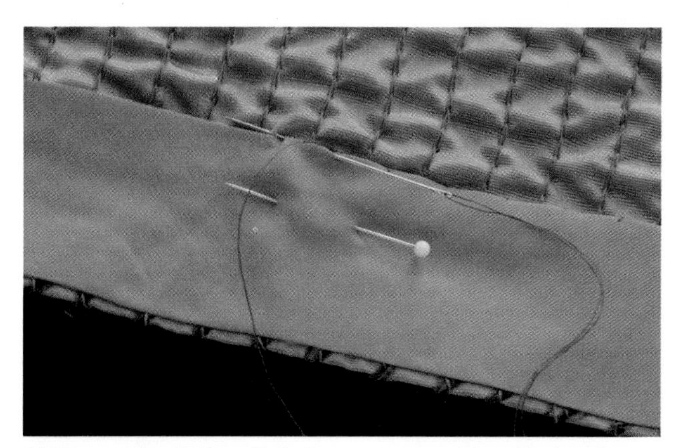

2) Press the facing lightly to wrong side; slipstitch or catchstitch in place.

How to Sew a Double-fold Hem

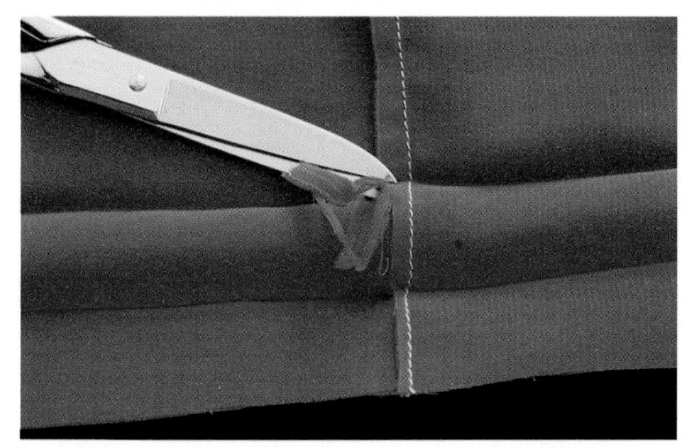

1) Trim fabric, allowing for twice the depth of the hem. Press half the hem allowance to wrong side; repeat, enclosing raw edge. Trim seam allowances in hem area to eliminate bulk.

2) Refold the hem allowance. Slipstitch the hem in place, catching one or two threads of outer fabric in each stitch.

How to Sew a Rolled Overlock Hem

Adjust serger to make rolled hem. Hold tail chain at beginning of hem; with right side of fabric facing up, stitch along hem edge and trim away the hem allowance with serger blades.

How to Sew a Topstitched Hem

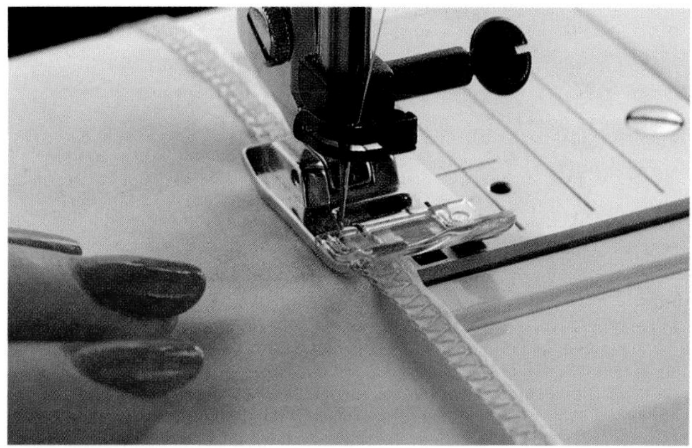

Fold and press hem allowance in place. Finish raw edge by overlocking it, or press under ¼" (6 mm). Machine-stitch hem.

Bustling Trains

After the wedding ceremony, the train of a bridal gown is usually bustled, or fastened up off the floor, allowing for easier movement. Bustling prevents damage to the gown and can also add interest to the back. There are two methods for bustling trains, each with a distinct look. Choose the method of bustling that complements the design of the gown and the fabric.

Overbustling is the most common method. The train fabric is brought up to the waistline in folds. Small thread loops on the train, and bustle buttons (page 33) or hooks at the waistline seam, secure the bustle. Overbustling may require only three buttons and loops, fastened at the center back and side seams. If the fabric is heavy or if the train is very long, you may distribute each fold into two smaller folds.

Underbustling is a process similar to overbustling, but the train fabric is folded under and brought up to the waistline, creating a different look. Ribbon loops and ties are used to hold the folds in place. An underbustled train does not place as much strain on the bride's back, making the bride more comfortable if the train is heavy because of its length or the weight of the fabric or beading.

Bustling is done when the gown is completed. With the bride-to-be wearing the shoes and petticoat that will be worn with the gown, mark the placement for any bustle buttons, hooks, loops, or ties. When bustling a train, it is not necessary to create an even hem; the primary purpose of bustling is to lift all or most of the train off the floor.

Overbustling (opposite) shortens the train by making folds in the fabric and securing them to the waistline on the right side of the gown. This is the quickest bustle to fasten.

Underbustling shortens the train by making folds in the fabric and securing them to the waistline between the train and the skirt lining.

How to Overbustle a Train

1) Measure the center back seam of train from the waistline seam to the floor, as indicated by red tape measure. Measure this distance from the edge of train, as indicated by blue tape measure; mark with pin.

2) Lift the center back seam at pin mark to waistline at center back. Adjust the fold so train is ½" to ¾" (1.3 to 2 cm) off the floor; pin to waistline seam as shown.

3) Fold and pin train at each side back seam, so sides of the train are off the floor ½" to ¾" (1.3 to 2 cm). Continue to fold and pin train as necessary between seams, to lift remaining train off the floor.

4) Check the drape of the train; if train is long or fabric is heavy, distribute each fold into two smaller folds. Each additional fold will require a bustle button or hook. Release bustle, pin-marking points on train and waistline.

5) Attach bustle buttons or hooks at waistline markings, stitching securely; to reinforce area, place small piece of interfacing under button or hook.

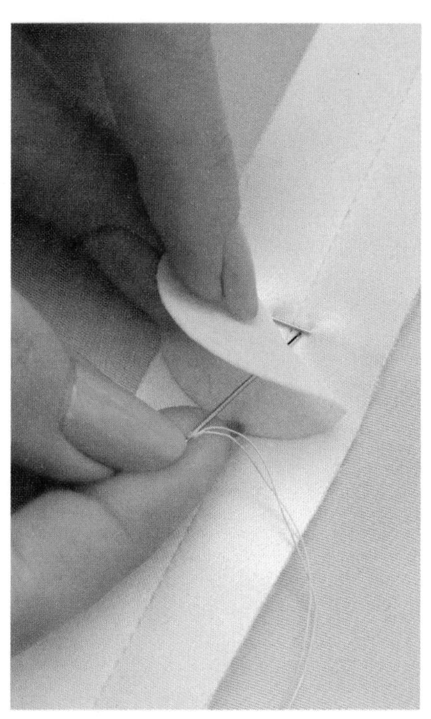

6) Thread needle with strong thread; knot ends together. Place small piece of interfacing on wrong side of train at marking for button loop. Insert needle at marking, next to seamline, through interfacing and train.

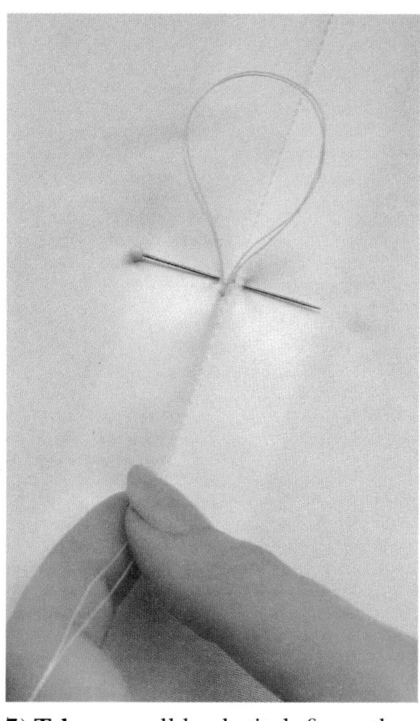

7) Take a small backstitch from the right side of the train; pull thread, leaving 1" to 2" (2.5 to 5 cm) loop.

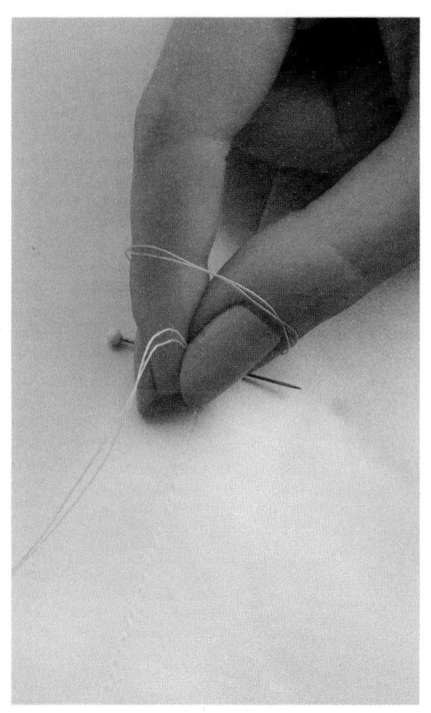

8) Insert fingers through the loop, and grasp thread as shown.

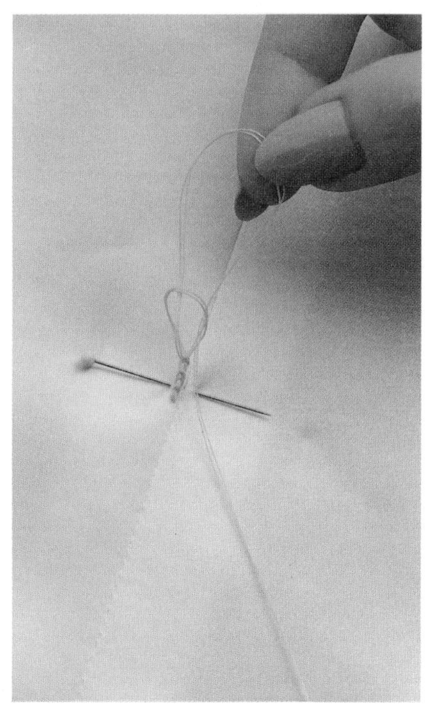

9) Pull the thread, tightening first loop and forming a second loop. Repeat, making a thread chain long enough to form a thread loop for fastening bustle button or hook.

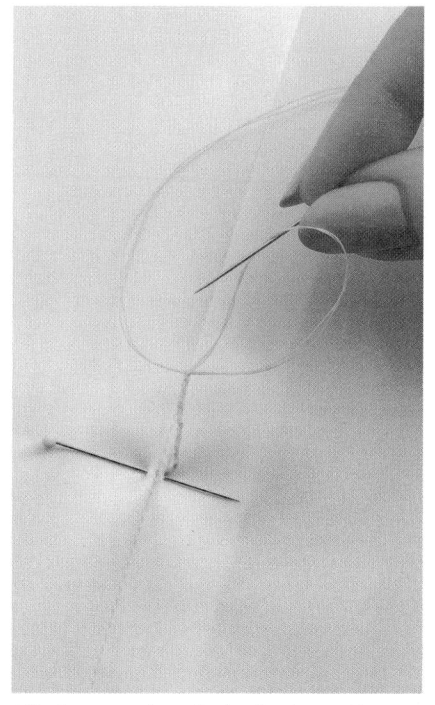

10) Secure the chain by inserting the needle and thread through the last loop.

(Continued on next page)

How to Overbustle a Train (continued)

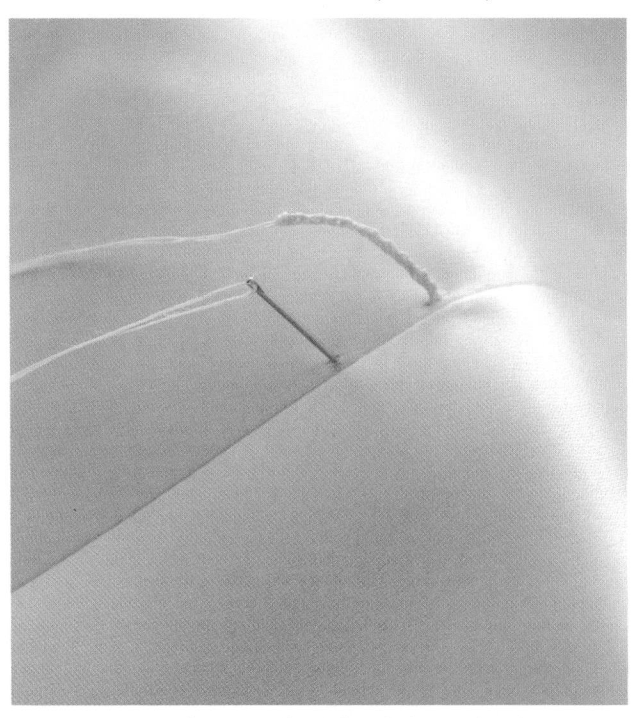

11) Insert needle to underside of the train, forming thread loop on right side, parallel to seam; secure thread on underside with several backstitches.

12) Hand-stitch lace appliqués in place, if desired, to conceal the bustle buttons or hooks. Bustle the train by fastening loops to buttons or hooks. Adjust folds of fabric for desired look.

How to Underbustle a Train

1) Measure the center back seam of train from the waistline seam to floor, as indicated by blue tape measure. Measure this distance from edge of train, as indicated by red tape measure; mark with pin.

2) Lift the center back seam at pin mark to waistline at center back; adjust the fold so train is ½" to ¾" (1.3 to 2 cm) off the floor; pin to the waistline seam as shown.

3) Fold and pin train at each side back seam, so sides of the train are off the floor ½" to ¾" (1.3 to 2 cm). Continue to fold and pin train as necessary between seams, to lift remaining train off the floor.

4) Release bustle, pin-marking points on train and waistline. Hand-stitch center of 15" (38 cm) length of narrow grosgrain ribbon to waistline at pin marks, between skirt lining and train; catch ribbon securely into waistline seam. Repeat to make remaining ties.

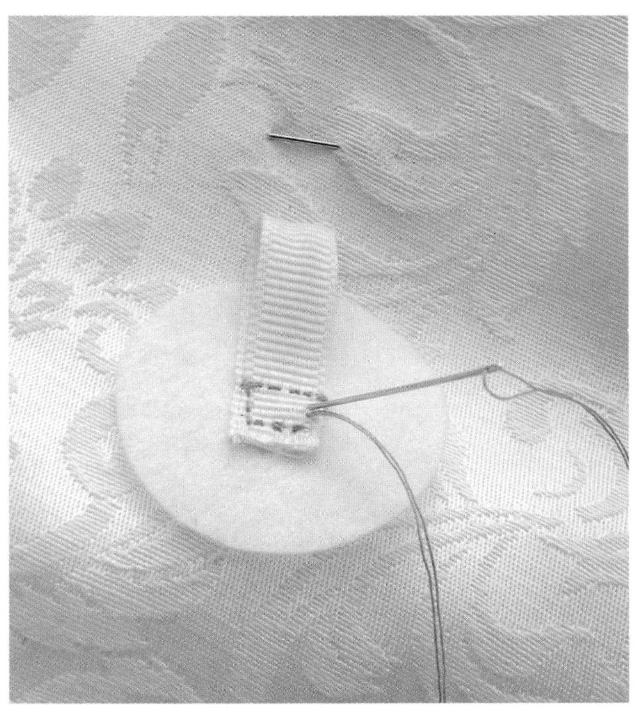

5) Cut 2½" (6.5 cm) length of grosgrain ribbon; fold in half, and stitch loop securely to underside of train, ½" (1.3 cm) below pin mark; reinforce area with small piece of interfacing, or attach ribbon loop to seam allowances. Repeat for remaining pin marks.

6) Insert ribbon ties through corresponding loops, and secure with a double bow. Adjust folds of fabric for desired look.

Special Techniques for Lace

Lace adds a glamorous, luxurious effect to a special gown. It can be used to embellish special-occasion dresses in many creative ways, from overall lace bodices to scattered lace appliqués on skirts and sleeves. For an opulent look, add beads and sequins to the lace.

One of the most elegant looks is the alençon bodice, completely covered in reembroidered lace. The alençon lace is shaped to follow the contours of the bodice for a seamless, continuous lace design.

Lace appliqués, easily attached with short running stitches, are often used to embellish bodice, skirt, and sleeve areas. Use lace appliqués to camouflage bodice seamlines or to emphasize the line of a basque waistline or a graceful Queen Anne neckline.

For elaborate lace designs on full skirts, cluster several appliqués together or scatter individual appliqués throughout the skirt. When planning the placement for appliqués on the skirt of a bridal gown, you may want to decide first on the placement of any bustle loops so the appliqués will be visible when the gown is bustled.

For the effect of lace openwork, trim away the fabric behind lace appliqués or edgings.

For added emphasis, use a lace edging along the curve of the neckline or to border the lower edge of the skirt and sleeves.

Alençon lace bodice (pages 103 to 105) is completely covered with lace that is shaped for a seamless effect, above. Or as shown below, a bodice may be embellished with lace appliqués (page 105).

Beading on lace (pages 108 and 109) adds highlights to special-occasion gowns. For ease in handling, the beading is completed as much as possible before the lace is applied to the garment.

Lace openwork (page 106) gives a sheer effect on sleeves and skirts.

Skirts may be trimmed with lace edgings as well as with scattered motifs. Apply lace edgings as on page 107.

Applying Lace to Bodices

There are two basic methods for applying lace to the bodices of gowns. In the first method, alençon lace is cut in one piece and shaped to the bodice. In the second method, lace appliqués and trims are applied in individual motifs to create one large design.

When the first method is used, the net background of the alençon lace is stretched and eased to fit the contours of the bodice with little or no cutting necessary. This eliminates seaming the lace at side seams, princess seams, and darts. The lace is hand-stitched to the garment and underlining. It can extend beyond the seams or finished edges of the garment. Or the lace edges can be stitched into the neckline, armhole, waistline, and center back seams. If the lace is stitched into the neckline or waistline seam, a lace edging is often applied after the garment is finished.

For an alençon lace bodice, purchase lace yardage wide enough and long enough to cover the bodice; to avoid buying excess lace, leave the muslin bodice with the shoulder seams unstitched, and take it with you when you purchase the lace. Most bodices can be covered with 1 to 1½ yd. (0.95 to 1.4 m) of 36" (91.5 cm) galloon lace. Individual motifs can be cut from the remnants and used for the skirt of the gown and to embellish headpieces.

In the second method, lace appliqués can be applied to a bodice for an overall effect or to create a focal point, such as a V on the bodice front. Position the appliqués along the finished edges or seams, or allow the appliqués to extend beyond them. If beading is desired, bead the appliqués before applying them to the bodice.

How to Make an Alençon Lace Bodice

1) Construct bodice as on pages 43 and 44, steps 1 to 3; spread on smooth, flat surface. Position lace over the bodice, aligning lace for efficient use; additional motifs may be applied to any areas not completely covered with yardage.

2) Thread-trace outline of bodice on the lace, if beading is desired. Apply beading within traced area (page 108).

3) Pin lace to bodice, starting at the center front and working with one hand underneath bodice to maintain its shape; thread tracing may no longer align with edge of bodice, because of shaping. Pin frequently, easing or stretching the net for smooth fit.

(Continued on next page)

How to Make an Alençon Lace Bodice (continued)

4) Continue pinning lace, working out to center back of the bodice. Repeat, working from center front to opposite side of center back. Remove thread tracing.

5) Trim lace around outer edges, allowing excess at this time; if lace will extend over the garment edge, trim around the motifs, applying liquid fray preventer to any cords of lace that are cut.

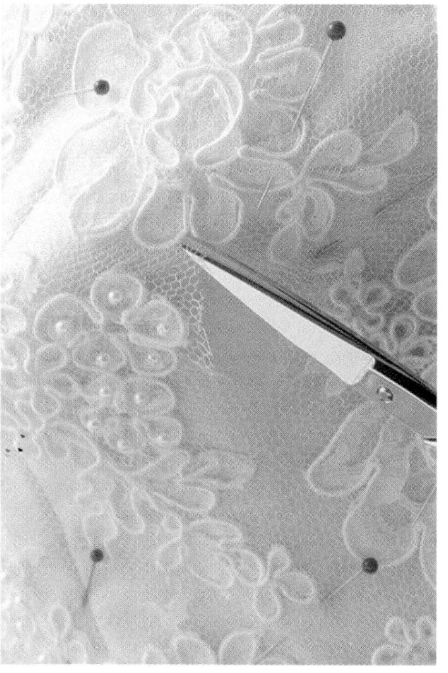

6) Baste the shoulder seams. Try on bodice, and check for puckers or folds; adjust lace, if necessary, for smooth fit. Net may be clipped in small areas to eliminate puckers; these clips will later be covered with lace motifs.

7) Trim lace that will be caught in seams even with the edge of the garment **(a).** Trim around motifs that will extend beyond edge **(b);** apply liquid fray preventer to any cords of lace that are cut.

8) Stitch shoulder seams, taking care not to catch lace in seams. Cut and pin additional motifs as necessary to conceal any clips, fill in design areas, or balance designs.

9) Hand-stitch lace to the bodice around motifs, using short running stitches; start at center front and work out. Stitch along inner edge of cord to conceal stitches. Leave loose any areas that will extend beyond edge or seam.

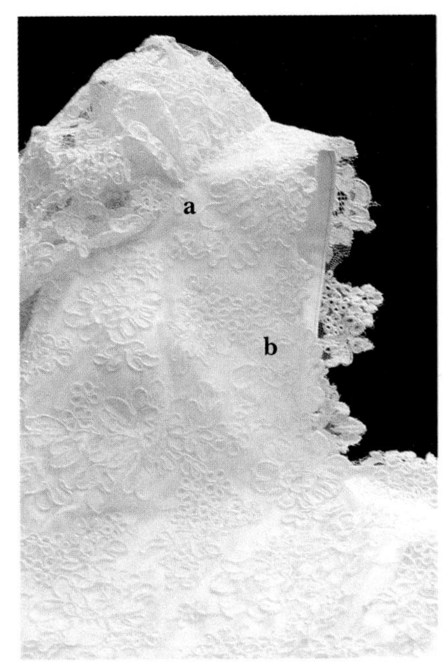

10) Assemble bodice lining, stitch neckline seam, and set in sleeves as on page 44, steps 5 and 6; catch lace in seam **(a)** or keep lace free to extend over seam or finished edge **(b)**.

11) Trim around the desired lace motifs, if lace extends over edges; apply liquid fray preventer to any cut cords, and secure edges. Add small lace motifs to fill in neckline as necessary.

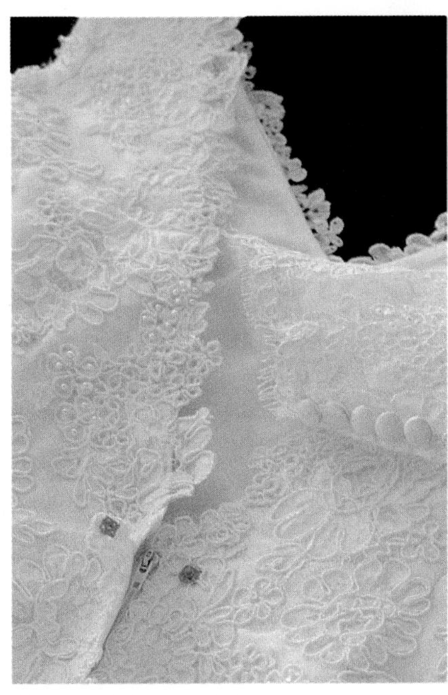

12) Apply lace edging to garment edges or seams. Apply clear snaps to secure motifs that extend over back closure. (Contrasting snap was used to show detail.)

How to Make a Lace Bodice Using Appliqués

1) Construct bodice as on pages 44 and 45, steps 1 to 3; stitch the shoulder seams. Pin prominent appliqués over princess seamlines or darts. Pin additional appliqués, arranging lace motifs for desired overall design.

2) Fill in the design areas with small lace motifs; apply liquid fray preventer to any cords of lace that are cut.

3) Secure lace as in step 9, opposite. Complete garment as in steps 10 to 12, above; in step 10, do not catch lace appliqués in seams.

Lace Openwork

Lace openwork is popular for sleeves and skirts of bridal gowns. Lace appliqués are stitched to the garment fabric, then the fabric is trimmed away. To stabilize the lace openwork, a layer of net or organza is often placed behind the lace. This is not necessary if the appliqués are small or if the garment area will not be subjected to stress.

Plan the placement of the lace openwork carefully, considering what will be exposed when the garment fabric is cut away. Avoid placing appliqués where lining seams or facings will be exposed. To determine the placement on skirts, pin the lace to the skirt after it is assembled and attached to the bodice. To determine the placement for lace openwork on sleeves, pin the sleeves in place or use the muslin sleeves of the test garment. It is easier to apply lace openwork before the sleeves are constructed.

How to Apply Lace Openwork

1) Cut an underlay of net or organza at least 2" (5 cm) larger than lace appliqué, and position on right side of garment; pin or baste in place. Center lace over underlay; pin or baste in place.

2) Hand-stitch lace in place, using short running stitches; stitch about 1/8" (3 mm) inside the edge of lace. Trim excess net or organza outside appliquéd area, using short scissors with sharp blades.

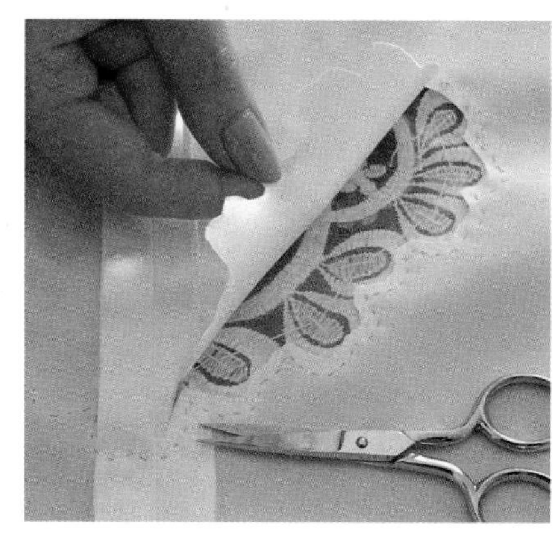

3) Trim fabric inside the appliquéd area, from wrong side, about 1/8" (3 mm) from stitching.

Lace Edging

Bridal gowns are often trimmed with lace edging at the lower edge of the hemmed skirt. These lace edgings usually range from 1" to 6" (2.5 to 15 cm). Most edgings will contour to the skirt edge with little or no clipping necessary. If you are using alençon lace, galloon lace can be cut to yield two strips of scalloped edging.

Edgings can be applied with the edge of the lace along the skirt hemline or extending beyond it. If the lace will be extended over the finished edge of the skirt, determine the placement of the lace before you hem the skirt; the lower edge of the lace should be ½" to ¾" (1.3 to 2 cm) from the floor. If the lace is extended too far beyond the hemline, the skirt can appear too short. If sheer areas are desired, small portions of the skirt can be cut away behind the lace.

Edgings may be applied by hand or by using a machine zigzag stitch. If you will be trimming away areas of the fabric, you may want to use a zigzag stitch to prevent the fabric from raveling.

How to Apply Lace Edging

1) Determine placement of lace on skirt. Hem skirt (pages 91 to 93). Pin lace to skirt, starting and ending at center back; clip and lap lace, if necessary. Use partial motifs at center back, if motifs do not match.

2) Apply additional appliqués, if desired, to create *godets,* or triangular clusters of motifs. Hand-stitch lace, using short running stitches, around each motif.

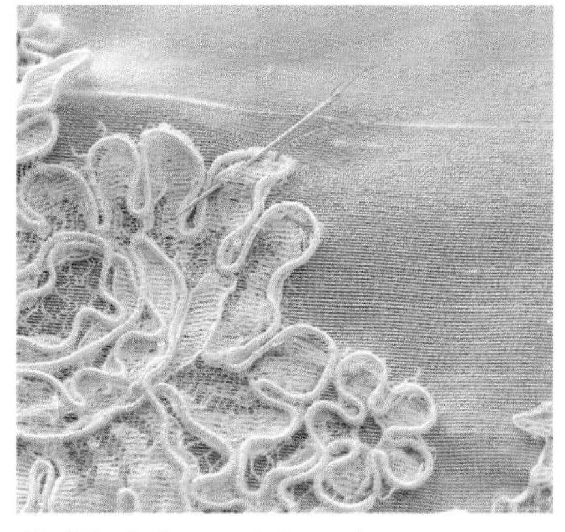

3) Stitch lace edging along upper edge, using short running stitches or machine zigzag stitch. If desired, trim fabric behind lace from wrong side, about ⅛" (3 mm) from the stitching, as in step 3, opposite.

Beading

Beading adds drama. Beads can be used to highlight lace when they are scattered lightly in an all-over pattern. Or they can create a focal point when applied heavily in a prominent design area. Hand beadwork is a sign of quality. It ensures that the beads will remain secure, even after dry cleaning.

Sequins may have pearl or iridescent finishes. Beads are available in many sizes, shapes, and finishes. Several types are often combined for beaded laces. Molded plastic beads that are permanently strung are quick to attach for long, continuous beading designs. Use purchased beaded dangle trims (page 31) to add instant drama to appliqués, or create your own dangle trims. When purchasing beads, make sure they can be dry-cleaned; some beads dissolve in dry-cleaning solution.

Beads usually follow the design lines of the lace and are often placed in clusters to embellish floral motifs. You may want to make photocopies of the lace and arrange the beads on the copies in various placements to determine the most attractive designs. The beads may be secured to the copies with rubber cement.

Hand beadwork is done using a double-threaded beading needle; a size 12 or 13 needle fits through most beads. Cotton-wrapped polyester thread is easy to handle and strong. Use short lengths of thread to prevent twisting and knotting, and reduce tangling by running the thread over beeswax.

Complete as much of the beading as possible before applying the lace to the garment. Bead the areas near the edges after the garment is completed. It is not necessary to place the lace in an embroidery hoop when beading; keep the stitches loose to prevent distortion. Secure the stitches frequently with backstitches, and do not carry the thread between lace motifs. Work from the center out.

Techniques for Applying Sequins

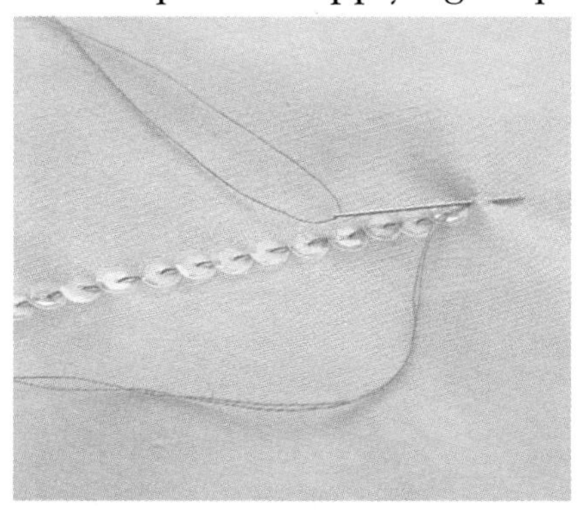

Continuous sequins. Bring needle up through a sequin and down at edge of sequin. Bring needle up to right side, less than half the width of sequin, and pick up next sequin; sequins will overlap.

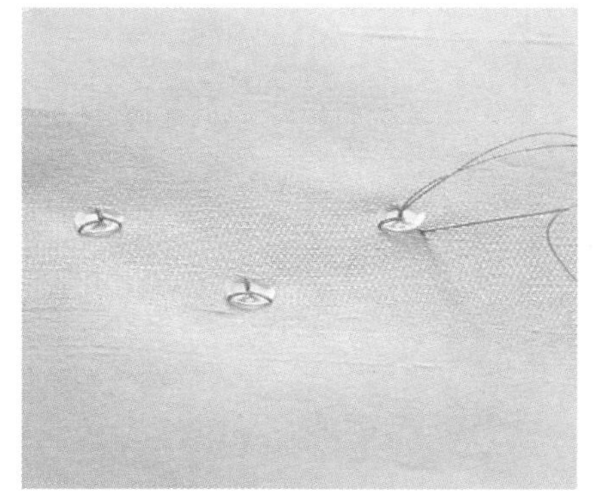

Scattered sequins. Take stitch up through center of the sequin and down at edge of sequin; repeat for two more stitches, spacing stitches at equal distances around sequin.

Scattered sequins with seed beads. Bring needle up through sequin, then through bead, on right side of fabric. Bring needle back through sequin, then down through fabric to wrong side.

Techniques for Applying Beads

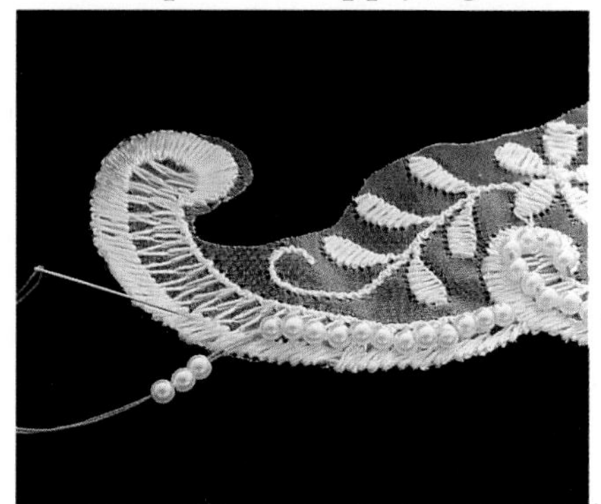

Continuous beads. Bring needle up to the right side through two to four beads; bring needle down to the wrong side next to last bead. Continue bringing needle up and down through the fabric, catching beads in each stitch.

Scattered beads. Bring needle up to the right side through a bead; taking a backstitch, bring needle down to wrong side close to the bead. Bring the needle forward to catch the next bead.

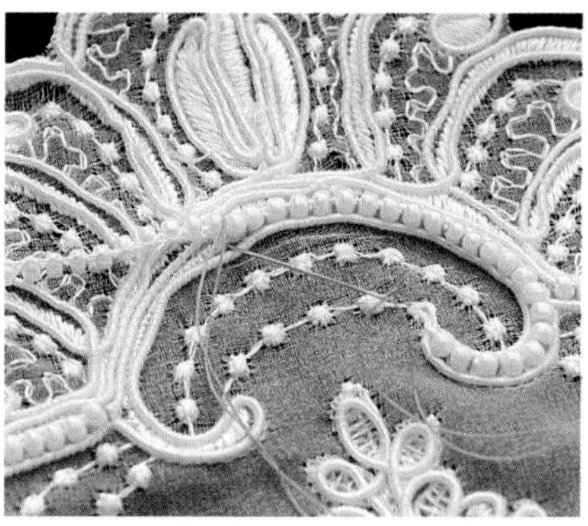

Prestrung beads. Stitch over base of bead strand, taking one stitch between beads, or take stitches at 1/4" to 3/8" (6 mm to 1 cm) intervals.

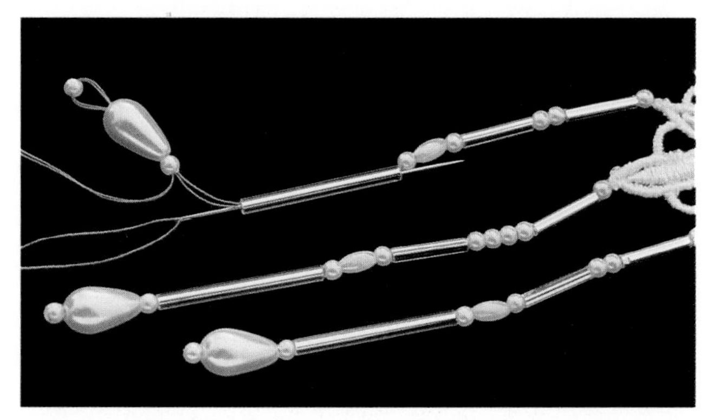

Hand-beaded dangles. Bring needle out through several beads at edge of the lace; the last bead, or the *stop,* is usually a small seed bead. Bring needle back through all beads except stop bead, then to wrong side of lace. Secure the threads on wrong side after each dangle stitch.

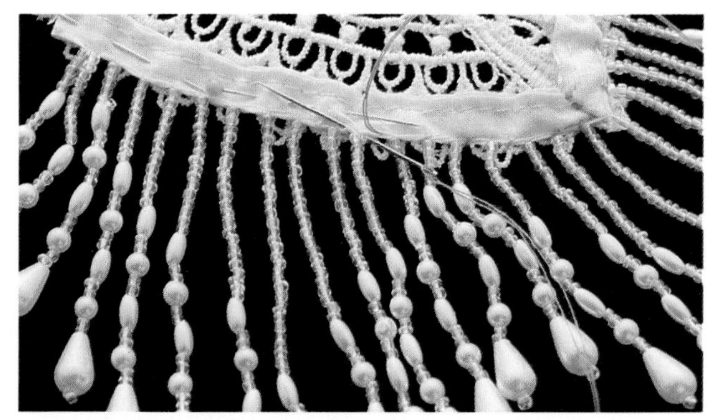

Purchased dangle trim. Pin tape of dangle trim to back of appliqué as desired. Whipstitch the tape in place, taking small stitches to conceal stitching.

Accessories

Headpieces & Hats

Headpieces and hats add the finishing touch to special-occasion outfits and are easy to cover with fabric. A veil may be attached to the headpiece or hat as on pages 118 to 121.

Headpieces are available in a variety of styles and may be a wire frame or buckram form; buckram picture and pillbox hats are available in several sizes. Choose a headpiece or hat style that is flattering to the shape of your face and the size of your head.

Headpieces can be covered with fabric and lace left over after sewing the gown. Most picture and pillbox hats can be covered with 5⁄8 yd. (0.6 m) of fabric.

Use a thick white craft glue or fabric glue for making headpieces and hats; a glue that sets up quickly is easiest to work with. Most embellishments, such as lace, appliqués, and pearls, can be secured with glue. You may want to hand-stitch pearl or flower sprays and net embellishments in place.

To provide a base for the embellishments, wire-frame headpieces are first covered with horsehair braid, available 3" and 6" (7.5 and 15 cm) wide. Elasticized button looping is used for securing plastic combs and bobby pins to a headpiece or hat; purchase a heavyweight button looping for maximum strength.

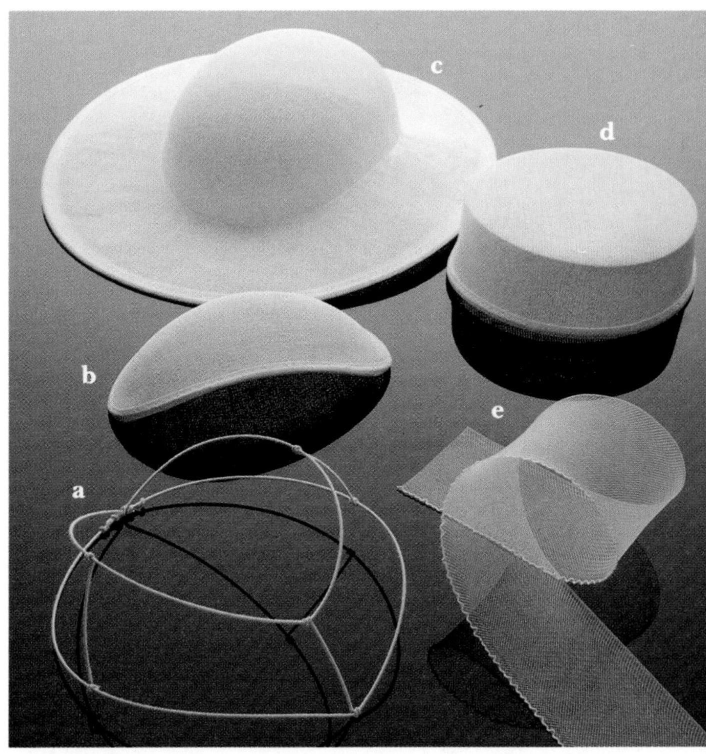

Headpieces and hats are available in a variety of styles, including wire frames **(a)**, buckram forms **(b)**, buckram picture hats **(c)**, and buckram pillbox hats **(d)**. Wide horsehair braid with a gathering cord on one side **(e)** is used for covering wire frames.

How to Cover a Wire-frame Headpiece

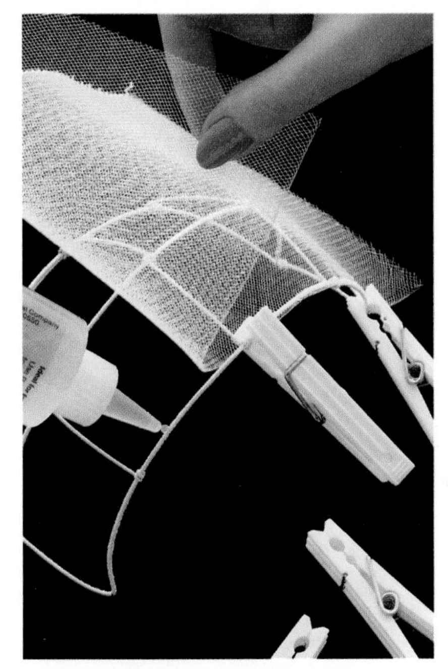

1) Cut horsehair braid 2" (5 cm) longer than frame. Glue uncorded edge of horsehair braid to widest outer edge of frame, applying dots of glue to frame. Secure with plastic clothespins, if necessary.

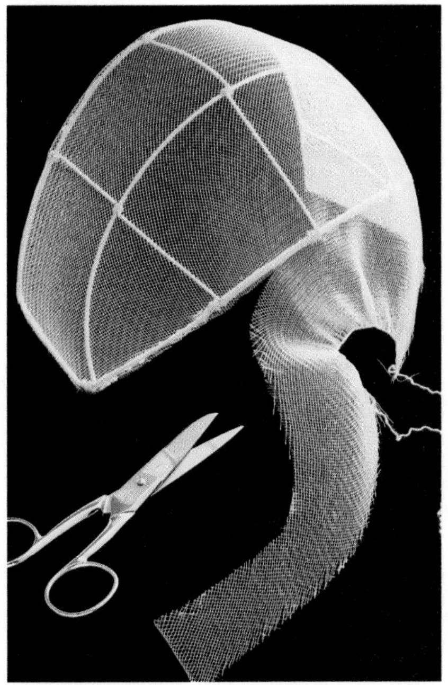

2) Pull on gathering cord to shape the horsehair braid to frame. Glue horsehair braid to the remaining outer edges. Allow glue to dry. Trim excess horsehair braid even with wire frame at edges.

3) Cover the frame with fabric, if desired, as on page 114, steps 1 and 2. Apply hair comb and lace, as in steps 3 to 6; cover the wire crosspieces with lace first, then fill in remaining areas.

How to Cover a Buckram Headpiece

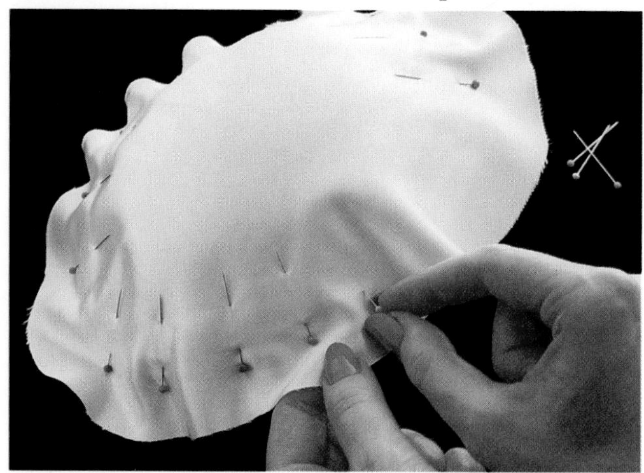

1) Cut a bias piece of fabric 1" to 2" (2.5 to 5 cm) larger than headpiece. Center fabric over top of headpiece, and secure with pins.

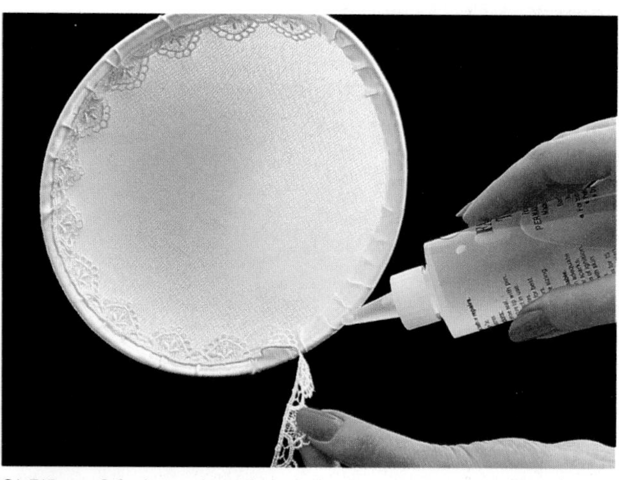

2) Wrap fabric to inside of the headpiece, and secure with glue; trim and clip fabric, and make small tucks for smooth fit. Glue lace trim over raw edge.

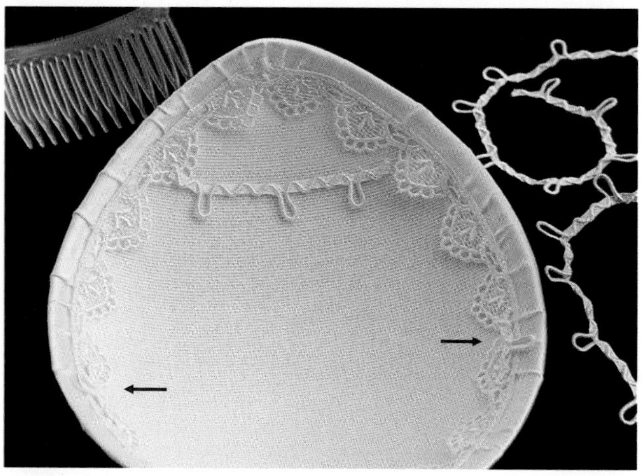

3) Cut a length of button looping slightly longer than hair comb; glue to inside of frame near front, with loops facing back of frame. Glue one loop of button looping at sides of headpiece (arrows).

4) Cut lace motifs; apply liquid fray preventer to the cut cords on lace. Arrange lace and any additional embellishments on the headpiece as desired; secure with glue or hand stitching.

5) Apply beads and sequins, if desired; using tweezers, dip bead in glue, and secure.

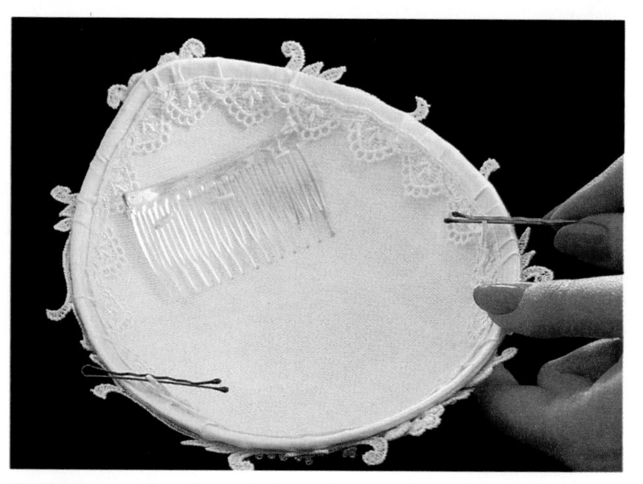

6) Slide teeth of comb into button looping at front of headpiece. Use loops at sides for securing the headpiece with bobby pins.

How to Cover a Buckram Pillbox Hat

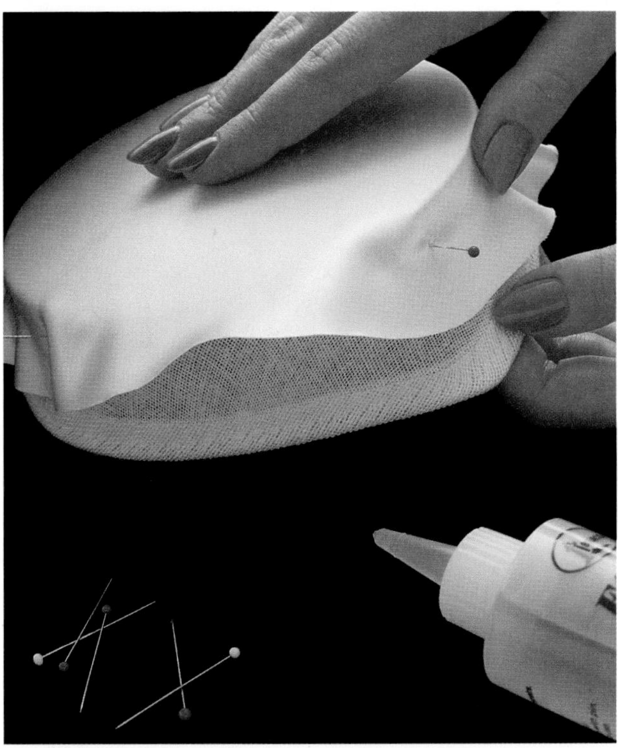

1) Cut fabric circle 1" to 2" (2.5 to 5 cm) larger than top of hat. Center fabric over top of hat, and smooth fabric over sides; secure with pins. Glue the fabric at sides, near top of hat, removing pins; allow to dry. Trim excess fabric.

2) Press pleats in bias strip of fabric, folding pleats so upper raw edge is concealed. Length of the pleated strip should be distance around hat plus 1" (2.5 cm) for overlap; width should be height of crown plus 1" (2.5 cm) for wrapping fabric to inside of hat.

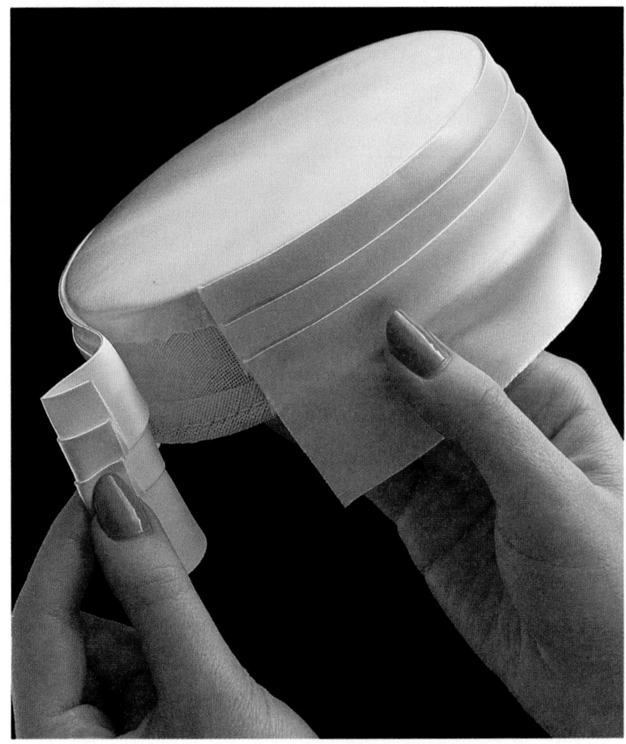

3) Glue pleated strip to crown; fold under one end, and lap over other end to conceal raw edge of fabric.

4) Wrap lower edge of fabric to inside of hat; secure with glue. Glue lace trim over raw edge. Complete headpiece, as in steps 3 to 6, opposite.

How to Cover a Buckram Picture Hat

1) Place hat on fabric, and mark from edge of brim a distance equal to width of the brim plus 1" (2.5 cm); repeat to mark around entire hat. Cut, following marked lines.

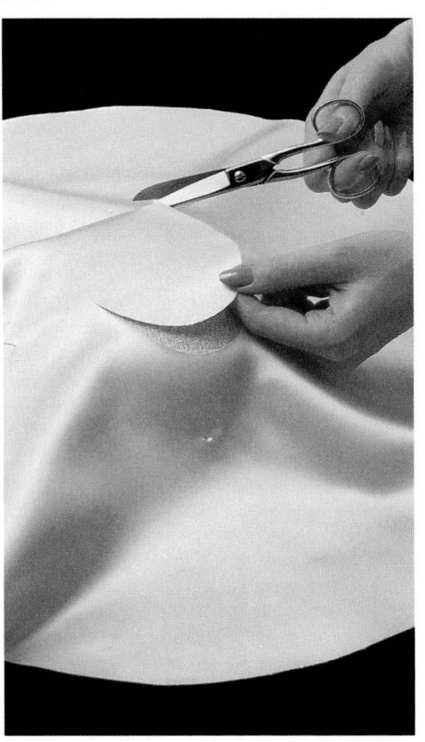

2) Center fabric right side up over hat; secure with pins into crown. Cut a hole in fabric at top of crown.

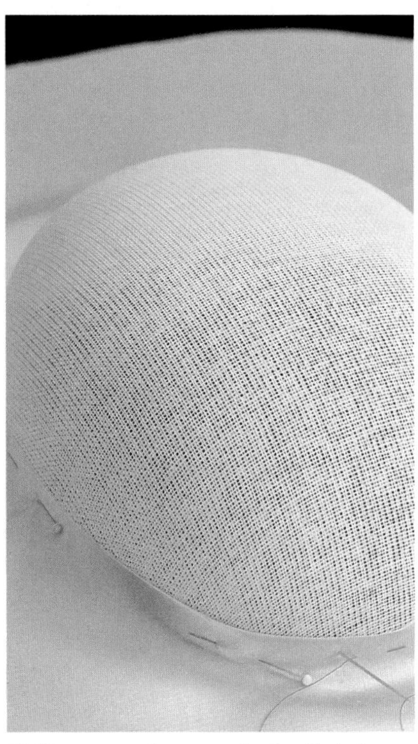

3) Remove pins; cut hole slightly larger. Repeat until fabric fits snug over crown and extends onto crown about 3/8" (1 cm). Pin in place; secure with hand stitching.

4) Wrap fabric around brim at center front; secure with pin at edge of crown. Repeat at center back, then at sides.

5) Make small pleats in fabric, working from side to center front and folding pleats so they face toward back of hat; secure each pleat with a pin.

6) Reverse the direction of the pleats at center front so pleats continue to face the back of the hat. Continue pleating to the center back.

7) Pleat remaining back section from side to center back. Hand-stitch pleats in place, about ½" (1.3 cm) from base of crown. Trim excess fabric.

8) Cut a bias piece of fabric slightly larger than crown. Smooth fabric around crown, and secure with pins; distribute fullness by making small tucks. Hand-stitch near base of crown. Trim excess fabric.

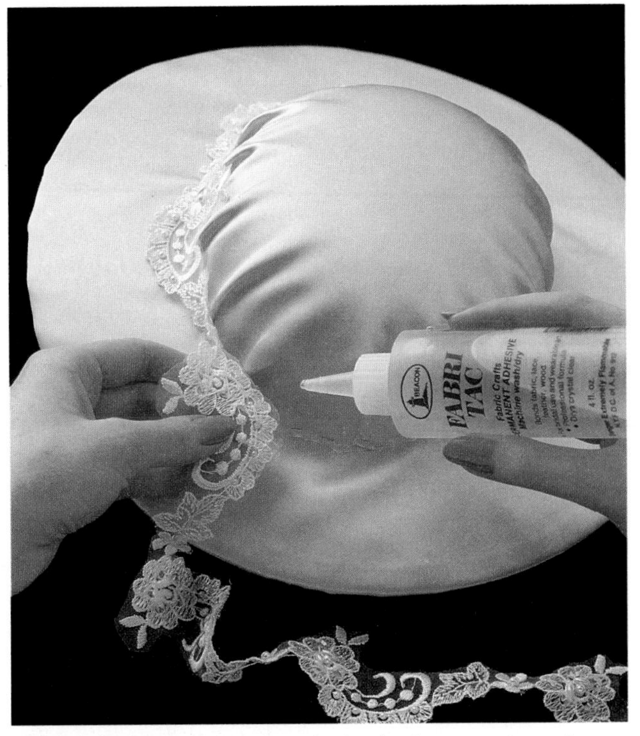

9) Glue lace trim or other desired trim over raw edges of fabric on inside and outside of hat. Hand-stitch or glue additional embellishments to hat as desired.

Bridal Veils

Bridal veils are easy to make, and the cost savings are substantial. Make the headpiece or hat to which the veil is attached, as on pages 113 to 117.

Try on several veils to determine the style and length that are most flattering. Many stores that carry veil and headpiece supplies have samples available. In general, the more elaborate the gown, the simpler the veil and headpiece.

Use the chart at right to determine the length of the veil. Also consider the formality of the wedding and the style of the back of the dress. If the veil is shorter than floor length, plan for it to end below the design features on the back of the dress, such as a low V neck, peplum, or bow; this will be more attractive visually, and the details will be visible through the sheer net.

Measure for the length of the veil from where it will be attached to the headpiece. The yardage of net required is equal to the combined length of the tiers; for a cascade veil with a pouf, add twice the height of the pouf.

Nylon illusion (page 26) is the most popular choice for bridal veils; it is generally available in 78" and 108" (198 and 274.5 cm) widths. Use the 78" (198 cm) width for shorter veils with less fullness; use the 108" (274.5 cm) width for floor-length and blusher veils.

An edge finish is not necessary on veils; for the easiest veil, simply cut rounded corners. For a rippled edge, stretch the net while stitching over fishline. Or for a decorative finish, apply ribbon, lace, or pearl cotton to the edges; for a ribbon finish, use 1/16" or 1/8" (1.5 or 3 mm) ribbon, so it lies smooth at curved edges. A cording foot is helpful for applying fishline and pearl cotton.

Cascade veil is gathered at the upper edge and sewn to the headpiece. Multilayered veils can be made by cutting two or three tiers; gather the tiers as one layer. A rippled edge finish is shown on this veil.

Bridal Veil Lengths

Description	Length
Shoulder or flyaway	Touches shoulders; usually worn with informal gowns.
Elbow	Touches elbows when arms are straight at the sides.
Fingertip	Touches fingertips when arms are straight at the sides.
Chapel	Falls about 2½ yd. (2.3 m) from headpiece.
Ballet or waltz	Falls to the ankles.
Cathedral	Falls about 3½ yd. (3.2 m) from the headpiece; usually worn with a cathedral train.

Cascade veil with a pouf is folded at the top and gathered 4" to 8" (10 to 20.5 cm) from the fold, to create the pouf. Depending on where the net is folded, this style can be a single layer or two tiers. A ribbon edge finish is shown on this veil.

Blusher veil drapes over the face and shoulders. The veil is not gathered the full width of the net, to allow the veil to drape at the sides. The blusher is folded back during the wedding ceremony. A pearl cotton edge finish is shown on this veil.

Three Ways to Edge-finish Bridal Veils

Rippled edge. Set the machine for narrow zigzag stitch. Place 30-lb. (13.6 kg) fishline 1/4" (6 mm) from edge of net. Stitch over fishline, stretching net as you stitch; overlap ends. Trim net close to stitching.

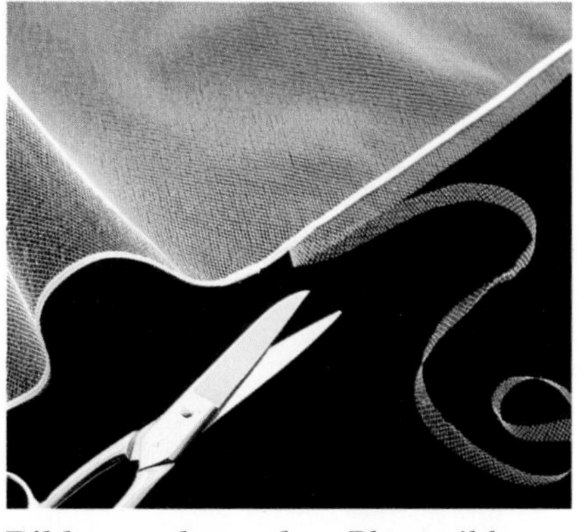

Ribbon or lace edge. Place ribbon or lace 1/4" (6 mm) from edge of net. Stitch, using straight or zigzag stitch; overlap ends. Trim net close to stitching.

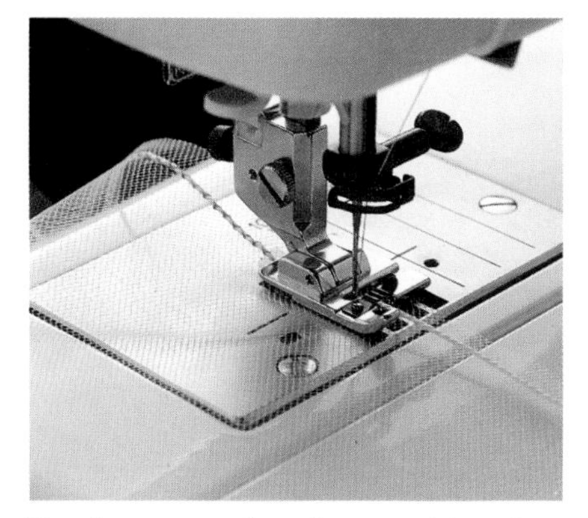

Pearl cotton edge. Set machine for narrow zigzag stitch. Position #5 or #8 pearl cotton 1/4" (6 mm) from edge of net. Stitch over the pearl cotton; overlap ends, and seal them with glue. Trim net close to stitching.

How to Make a Cascade Veil

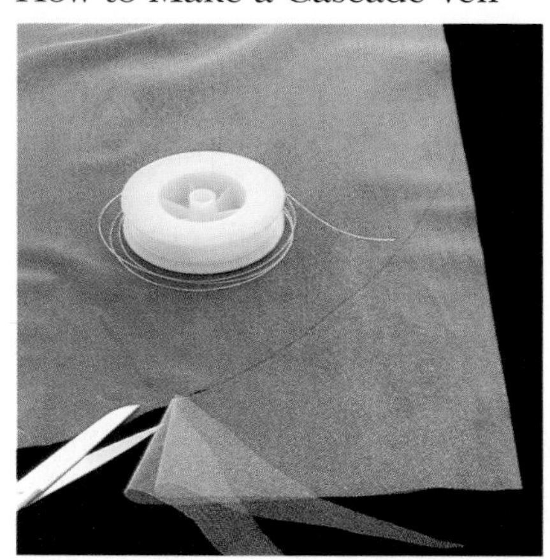

1) Cut net to desired length; fold in half lengthwise. Cut rounded corner on cut edges of lower corner. Apply trim (page 119), if desired.

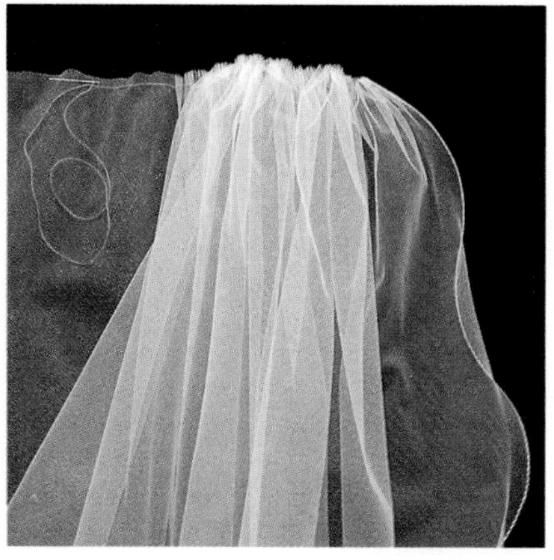

2) Stitch a gathering row about 1/4" (6 mm) from upper edge of net; hand-stitch, using double thread.

3) Make headpiece (pages 113 and 114). Gather net to fit headpiece; hand-stitch in place.

How to Make a Cascade Veil with a Pouf

1) Determine the height of pouf desired by folding a length of net; hand-gather 4" to 8" (10 to 20.5 cm) from folded edge. Position gathered net at the back of headpiece; adjust height of pouf.

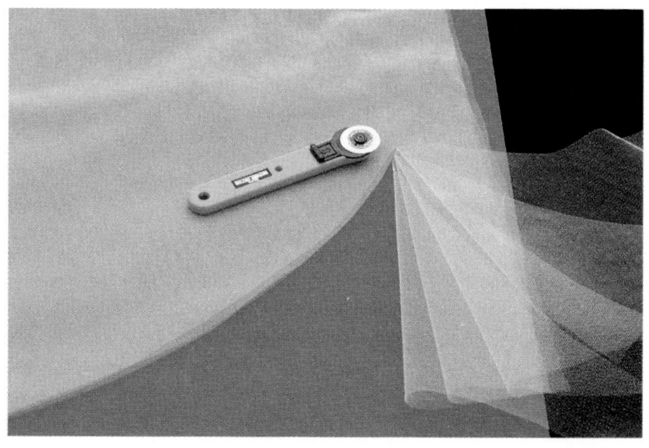

2) Cut net; cut length is equal to combined length of each tier plus twice the height of pouf. Fold net in half lengthwise; for two-tier veil, fold in half again, crosswise. Cut rounded corner on cut edges of lower corner.

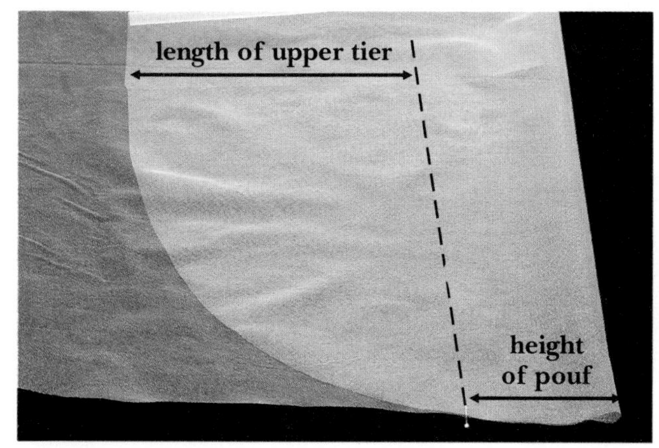

3) Fold net at desired height of pouf and length of upper tier; on both sides of veil, place pins at bottom of pouf on lower tier, near edges. Omit step 4 if ribbon or lace trim is not desired.

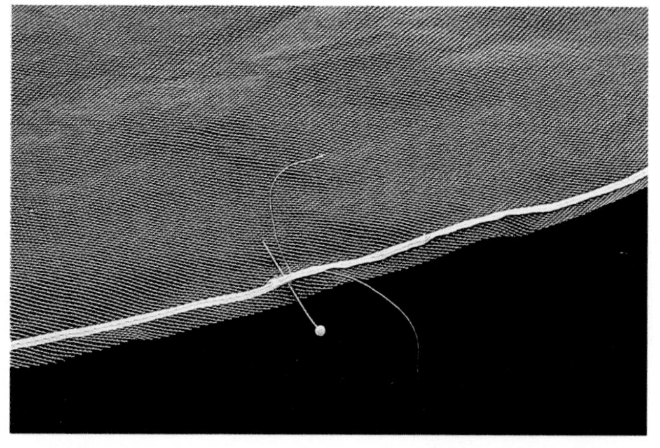

4) Apply ribbon or lace trim, as on page 119, to right side of lower tier, between pin marks. Apply trim to reverse side of pouf and upper tier; this will be on right side of veil when veil is worn.

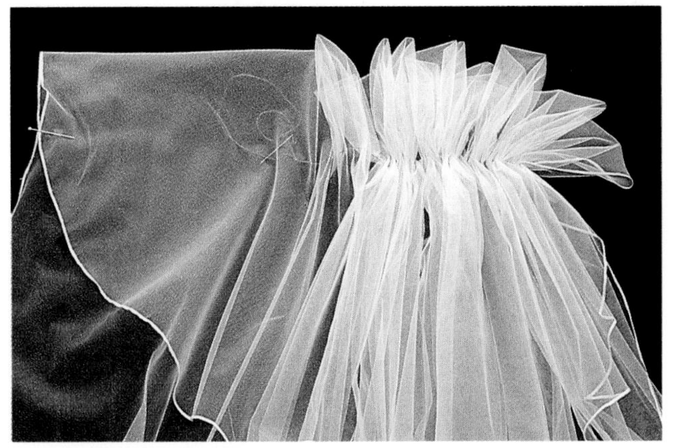

5) Refold veil as in step 3. Using double strand of thread, hand-stitch a gathering row through both layers, with distance from folded edge equal to the height of pouf.

6) Make headpiece (pages 113 and 114). Gather net to fit headpiece; hand-stitch in place. Adjust pouf by separating layers of net.

How to Make a Blusher Veil

1) Determine combined length of front blusher and back tier, measuring from where veil will be attached to headpiece; blusher should fall at bustline. Cut net to this length.

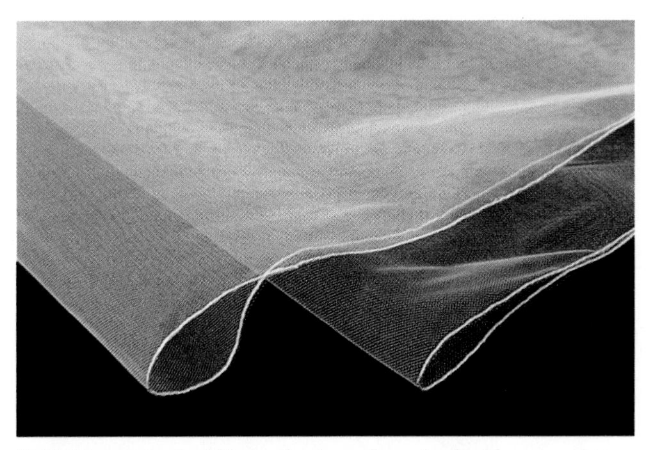

2) Fold net in half lengthwise, then in half crosswise. Cut rounded corner on cut edges of lower corner. Apply trim (page 119), if desired.

3) Hand-stitch a 72" (183 cm) gathering row in center portion of veil, with distance from front edge equal to length of blusher; this leaves an ungathered area at each side of veil.

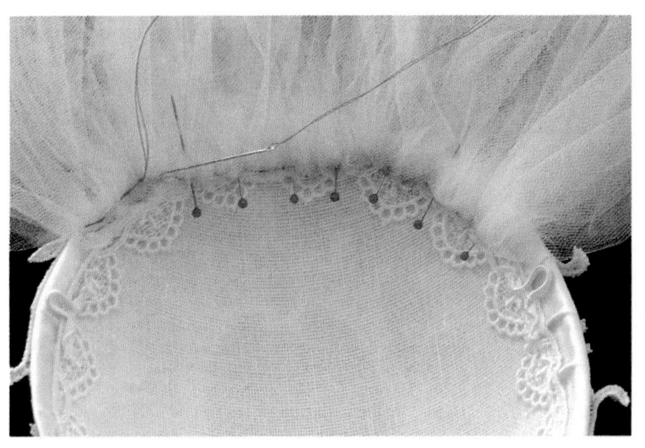

4) Make headpiece (pages 113 and 114). Gather net to fit headpiece; hand-stitch in place.

Cancan Petticoat

Make a full cancan petticoat, using an A-line skirt pattern. A spandex upper panel, with an invisible zipper and elasticized waistband, fits smoothly and comfortably at the waist and hips. Two layers of cancan net are used for greater fullness. A lower ruffle provides the majority of the fullness, and a full-length ruffle, starting at the hips, supports and keeps the flare of the gown smooth. The amount of net used can be varied to achieve the desired fullness.

The instructions that follow are for a petticoat with a 10" (25.5 cm) upper panel. Cut the upper panel from spandex power net or two-way stretch swimsuit fabric. For the lower petticoat, use an A-line skirt pattern in your normal size. Cut the lower petticoat from taffeta. The finished length of the petticoat should be about 1" (2.5 cm) shorter than the gown.

The ruffles are made from strips of 54" (137 cm) cancan net (page 27); this type of net provides the best support and does not lose its crispness in handling or laundering. For a very full petticoat, cut six strips of net for each layer; if less fullness is desired, cut four or five strips for each layer. A full-length petticoat with six strips for each layer requires about 10 yd. (9.15 m) of 54" (137 cm) net.

How to Make a Cancan Petticoat

1) Make pattern for upper panel by marking a line equal to one-half of the hip measurement. Mark a parallel line, equal to one-half of waist measurement, centered 10½" (27.8 cm) above first line. Connect lines for side seams.

2) Fold paper on waistline, and mark a parallel line 1" (2.5 cm) from fold for elastic casing; trace angled sides. Mark the grainline on pattern for maximum stretch of the fabric.

3) Cut one panel front from spandex power net or two-way stretch swimsuit fabric, using pattern. Cut two panel backs by folding pattern in half and adding ⅝" (1.5 cm) seam allowances for center back seam.

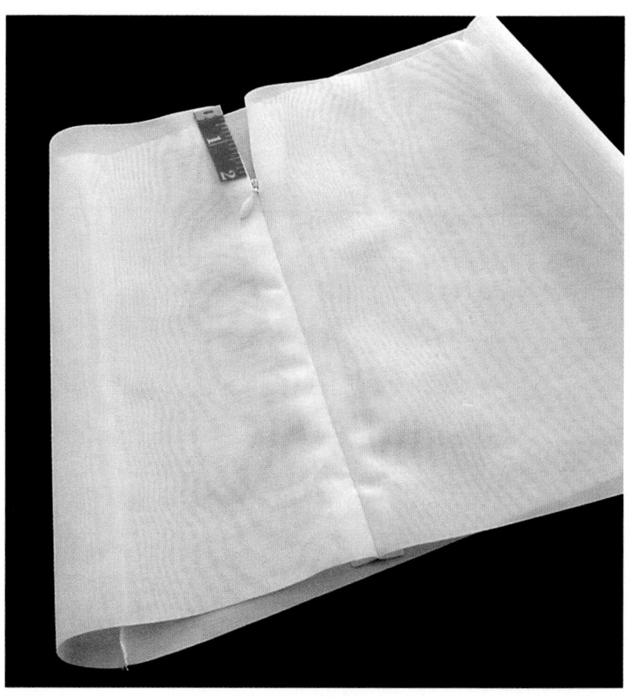

4) Insert invisible zipper (page 82) in center back seam of upper panel; position zipper tab 2" (5 cm) from the upper edge of the fabric. Stitch ¼" (6 mm) side seams.

(Continued on next page)

5) Fold 1" (2.5 cm) to wrong side on the upper edge; stitch close to raw edge, stretching as you sew or using zigzag stitch, to make casing. Cut ¾" (2 cm) elastic for comfortable fit at the waist. Insert elastic in casing; secure by stitching across ends. Attach hook and eye.

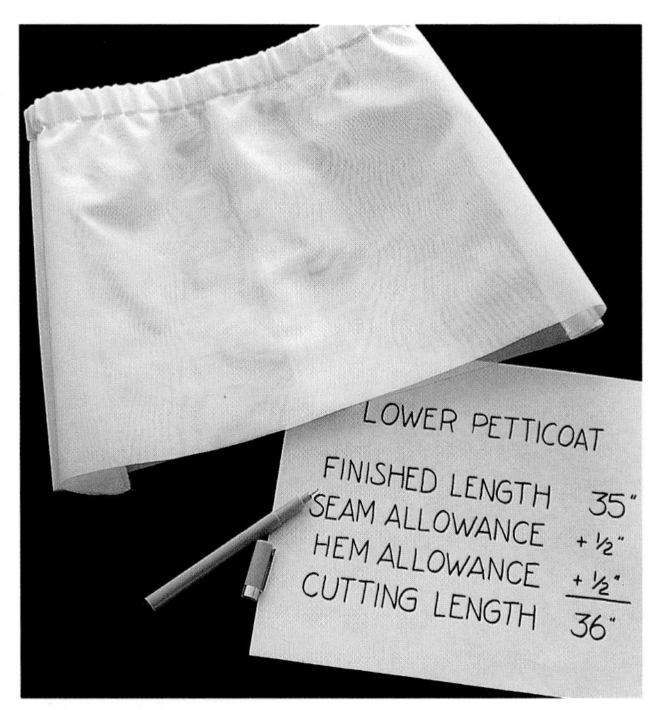

6) Try on upper panel, and determine desired length of lower petticoat, measuring from side of panel; add to this measurement ½" (1.3 cm) for upper seam allowance and desired hem allowance.

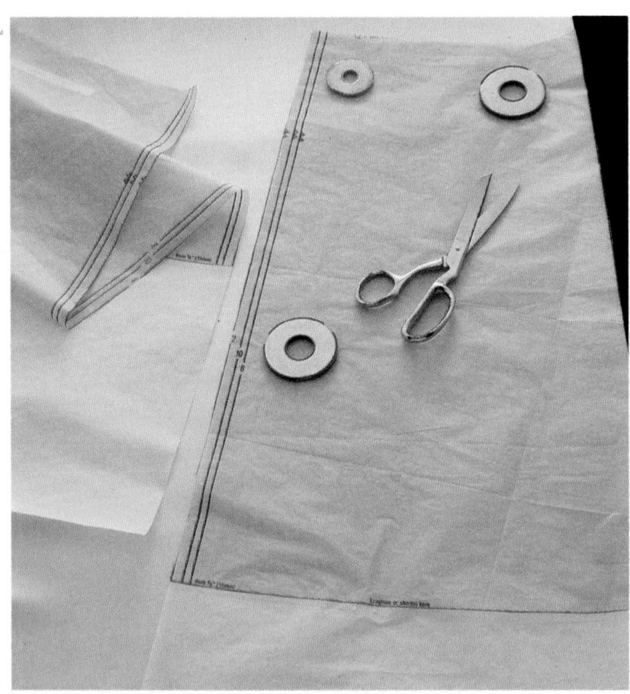

7) Cut top of A-line skirt pattern so it is at least 2" to 3" (5 to 7.5 cm) larger than hip measurement. Adjust the length of the skirt pattern as necessary for desired finished length of petticoat. Cut lower petticoat from taffeta, using adjusted pattern.

8) Stitch seams of lower petticoat. Divide upper panel and lower petticoat into fourths; pin-mark. Pin the sections, with right sides together and raw edges even, matching pin-marks. Stitch ½" (1.3 cm) seam, stretching upper panel to fit lower petticoat. Hem lower petticoat as desired (page 91).

9) Stitch four to six 25" × 54" (63.5 × 137 cm) strips of net together; fold in half to make 12½" (31.8 cm) folded strip. Stitch a gathering row by zigzagging over a strong cord, ⅝" (1.5 cm) from fold.

10) Mark a line, using a water-soluble marking pen, 12½" (31.8 cm) from lower edge of petticoat. Divide net and petticoat at marked line into fourths; pin-mark. Gather and pin net to right side of petticoat, matching pin marks and aligning fold of net with marked line. Stitch over gathering cord.

11) Stitch four to six strips of net together for the upper ruffle, with length of strips equal to finished length of the lower petticoat. Stitch a gathering row ⅝" (1.5 cm) from the upper edge. Divide net and petticoat into fourths; gather net to petticoat, aligning edge with seam. Stitch over gathering cord.

12) Compress petticoat for storage; restore fullness by shaking the petticoat out. For additional fullness, separate layers of net in lower ruffle.

Index

Creative Publishing international, Inc
offers a variety of how-to books. For
information write:
Creative Publishing international, In
Subscriber Books
5900 Green Oak Drive
Minnetonka, MN 55343